Can the Greeks Cook!

By

Fannie Venos and
Lillian Prichard

ECHO POINT BOOKS & MEDIA, LLC
Brattleboro, Vermont

Published in 2024 by Echo Point Books & Media
Brattleboro, Vermont
www.EchoPointBooks.com

Can the Greeks Cook!
ISBN: 978-1-64837-389-3 (casebound)
       978-1-64837-390-9 (paperback)

Cover design by Kaitlyn Whitaker

Cover image: Mediterranean Food by antlexx,
courtesy of Shutterstock

DEDICATED
TO MY SISTER,
ARGIE,
FOR HER PATIENT HELP IN
TESTING THE RECIPES
IN THIS BOOK.

Contents

	Page
DEDICATION	iii
ACKNOWLEDGMENTS	vi
FOREWORD	vii
INTRODUCTION	xi
GREEK SUPERSTITIONS	xiii
SAUCES	1
SOUPS	4
CHEESES	8
CHEESE AND MILK RECIPES	9
EPIPHANY DAY	13
SALADS	15
VEGETABLES	19
MEAT RECIPES	43
FOWL RECIPES	67
GREEK EASTER FOOD CUSTOMS	72
FISH AND SEAFOOD RECIPES	75
GREEK WEDDING TRADITIONS AND CUSTOMS	86
GREEK PASTRIES RECIPES	89
RECIPE FOR GREEK COFFEE	115
INDEX TO RECIPES	117

Acknowledgments for Recipes

Mrs. Charles Simeon
Mrs. Dorothy Kisaris
Miss Lula Cardullias
Mrs. Stephen Koundouriotis
Mrs. George Pareskevas
Mrs. Dona Constantinou
Mrs. Harry Malamatos
Mrs. Tony Giallourakis
Mrs. D. Allisandratos
Mrs. Angelo Tsardoulis
Mrs. Katherine Kelkanteris
Mrs. Christopher Rallis
Mrs. Katina Vamvakias
Miss Dora Economopoulos
Mrs. Kaliope Koutsourais
Mrs. Themalina Angel
Mrs. Chris Sarandon
Mrs. James Peterson
Miss Caliope Manias

Mrs. George Mavros
Mrs. George Esfakis
Mrs. C. G. Mitchell
Mrs. Nick Cretekos
Mrs. Peter Velousis
Mrs. Nick Marlemes
Mrs. Mike Nicholis
Mrs. Tom Canacaris
Mrs. Gus Cocoris
Mike Melissas
Mrs. Peter Nichols
Mrs. Tina Kesaris
Miss Kay Melissas
Mrs. G. Rezoulis
Mrs. Chris Esfakis
Miss Lula Houllis
Mrs. Jim Ergas
Mrs. John Panos

FOREWORD
A Note About Terms and Ingredients

Delve into the enticing culinary delights of Greek cooking and you are immediately taking a trip back in time. Greek food is borne of a rich tapestry of local ingredients combined to produce traditional meals that never fail to satisfy. Whether you are entering new taste territory or increasing your selection of Greek recipes, familiarity with the methods, terms, and ingredients will aid your journey.

First, a little terminology. Greek cuisine is comprised of joining basic ingredients found in the northeastern Mediterranean using a variety of common cooking methods. There is the stovetop casserole, or *kapama*, usually flavored with a sweet or spicy tomato sauce. The meatless casserole is known as *lathera* or *ladera*. Poaching—*pose* (pronounced po-ZAY)—is also common, as is stewing—*stifatho* or *stifado,* or *yahni* if the stewing is ragout style. *Sote* is sauté, while *pane* (pronounced pay-NAH) is breaded and fried; *tiganita* denotes skillet frying, while *skharas* is grilling. In the oven, *ogkraten* is anything baked in a cheese sauce and *sto fourno* is baking or oven roasting. Pickled foods are *toursi;* purée or mash is *poure.*

A general knowledge of the major Greek ingredients can be useful regardless of whether you are creating or consuming a Greek delicacy. At the top of the list is, of course, olive oil (*elaiolado*), which comes in many local varieties from the native trees; it is an essential ingredient for everything from spanakopita to seafood saganaki. Feta cheese can be made from cow, goat, or sheep's milk and its tangy, salty flavor adds a distinct flourish to a wide variety of Greek dishes. Olives (*elia*) are ever-present in Greek dining, especially the national favorite, kalamata, which is often marinated and stuffed with herbs and spices. Greek yogurt (*yiaourti*), though not originating in Greece, plays a massive role in present-day Greek cooking, adding a velvety, slightly sour contrast to many fruit and vegetable presentations. Singular to the Greek island of Chios, mastic—the crystallized resin from pistachio trees—adds its pine-like aroma and sweet, fruity taste to many desserts and candies, and also infuses the favorite regional liqueur *mastiha.*

Foreword

The Greeks are devotees of using fresh herbs in their cooking, and the following list of the most common herbs and their Greek names will help the diner and chef parse many a Greek recipe.

Common Name	Greek Name	Common Name	Greek Name
Aurugula (Rocket)	Roka	Oregano (Greek)	Rigani, origano
Basil	Vasilikos, basiliko	Parsley	Maïdanos, miantano
Bay Leaf	Daphni	Purslane	Glistritha
Dill	Anithos	Rosemary	Thentrolivano
Fennel (leaves)	Maratho	Sage	Faskomilo
Majoram	Mantzourana	Savory	Throubi

Regardless of whether you are a tourist or a creator in the land of Greek cooking, *Can the Greeks Cook!* by Fannie Venos and Lillian Prichard provides a thorough introduction to all the traditional recipes in the Greek culinary repertoire.

Introduction

THE recipes included in this book are a cross section of Greek recipes from many sections of Greece. They are the favorite recipes brought to America by Greeks from the Dodecanese Islands, from Athens, from Aegina, from Crete and many other parts of Greece.

To these many cooks who have retained their love of Greek cooking, and who so generously aided us in donating their favorite recipes, we extend our heartfelt appreciation.

While our contributions came from friends in many cities of the United States, the majority of them came from residents of our home town, Tarpon Springs, Florida. The Greek colony of this city is well-known throughout the United States and is one of the principal attractions on the West Coast of Florida.

In this picturesque colony, the traditions and customs as well as the food habits of Greece are preserved with all the warmth and beauty of Greece.

We trust that the recipes in this book will prove an enjoyable experience to those who try them.

THE AUTHORS.

Greek Superstitions

STATISTICS have proven that people the world over are a superstitious lot. However, the Greek people are among those classed as the most superstitious. From infancy, their children are taught to beware of those things which bring bad luck, and to recognize those which will bring good luck.

When a baby is born, one of the first things placed on the child's garments is a bit of gold. Sometimes an earring, a ring, or a gold piece. Superstition has it that on the first three days of the child's life, the fairies come to call on the infant and decide its fate. If there is gold on the baby, they will be pleased and predict only good things.

The babies come in for a bit more of strange superstition, for when a newborn infant is first seen, the onlooker must follow compliments and comments with a "puffing" into the child's face. The reason for this strange action is based on the belief that none knows if they have the evil eye, and the power to transmit it to another; therefore the "puffing" dispels any "evil eye" which the well-wisher may have cast upon the child. Needless to say this is somewhat disconcerting to the reposing infant.

In the event that a mother returns from a stroll with her baby and notices that the child is restless or listless, she racks her brain to remember who looked at the baby and did not "puff." In this case, if the "evil-eye" has been cast, there are old-timers who have the power to remove the offending influence.

While on the subject of babies, a favorite trick is to sprinkle salt on the head of an expectant mother to determine the sex of the baby-to-be. When the unsuspecting victim is not noticing, sprinkle a bit of salt on her head, and then sit back and observe the movements of her hands. If she raises her hands towards her head immediately after this, the child will be a girl. If her hands go towards the lower part of the body, the baby will be a boy. This trick was tried on the writer, who unknowingly pushed her hair back at first, then in the next gesture straightened her skirt. Believe it or not, when the baby arrived, it wasn't one but two. A girl at first—then a boy. There must be something to it after all.

Tuesday is considered a very unlucky day by both men and women. No out of the ordinary task is begun on this day. A dress cut out on Tuesday will invariably turn out to be a "lemon." One way to get around this is to cut out part of the dress Monday night. This breaks the spell.

In Tarpon Springs, which is the home port of the famous Greek Sponge fleet, the sponge divers have their share of superstitions which are generally observed by Greek seamen. No whistling is allowed on deck while a diver is down below. It is considered bad luck. A boat will never sail on Tuesday, and if there is a red-headed woman on the docks, when the boat prepares to leave, they will remain in port until she leaves. There was, up until a few months ago, before her death, an old lady known as the "woman in black", who was supposed to have the power of casting evil spells. If she were seen on the docks as a boat prepared to depart, they would cancel the trip, and depart the next day.

Also on board these boats the seamen carry an ikon of St. Nicholas, patron saint of all seamen; and burn a holy light before it throughout the entire trip. Should it go out, it betokens ill luck.

In the Greek Orthodox churches at Easter time, a large flower-bedecked catafalque is used to denote the bier of Christ. It is considered good luck to crawl beneath this catafalque, first from the lengthwise part and back under the crosswise section, making the sign of the cross. This brings good luck throughout the year. In connection with the Easter services, it is considered good luck to carry home a lighted candle from the Resurrection services, held always at midnight on Saturday. These candles are used to smoke the sign of the cross above the entrance to the house to ward off evil during the year.

There are many other superstitions which are practiced day after day, until they become a habit with those who do them. It is considered bad luck to pass the salt from one person's hand to another; sweeping beneath a person's feet or stepping over a person's legs denotes they will be an old maid or a bachelor; never brush your hands at the conclusion of a meal, because it denotes that the food just consumed "benefits none but the devil." The first articles moved into a new home are a new broom and a loaf of bread to insure a clean home and a full larder.

There are no doubt many more, which are unknown to the writer; however, these are the outstanding ones wherever there are Greek people.

SAUCE RECIPES

GARLIC SAUCE
"Skorthalia"

"This highly seasoned sauce is rated as one of the top delicacies in the Greek kitchen; however, in order to perfectly enjoy it, a suggestion that everyone at the table partake of it is highly advisable. The strong after-fumes will be less noticeable if this precaution is taken. Not to be eaten before the theatre or a social gathering."

5 cups mashed potatoes (about 3 lbs.)
2 garlic heads (med.)
2½ cups pure olive oil
3 egg yolks
⅔ cup vinegar
½ cup water
1 tbsp. salt

Clean and mash garlic cloves with 1 tbsp. salt in a large

"gthi" (Greek garlic bowl, which resembles a pharmacists' mortar and pestle).

Continue mashing until thin and smooth. While this is being done, cook and mash potatoes until fluffy. Use electric mixer if possible to obtain creamy consistency. Add garlic paste to potatoes continuously beating. Add olive oil very slowly until completely absorbed. Add vinegar and beat thoroughly. Add egg yolks and salt to taste. Continue beating until smooth paste is formed (about 10 min.).

If stronger garlic flavor is preferred, use only 4 cups of potatoes. If thinner sauce is desired, use an additional ⅓ cup water. Serve with fish, boiled shrimp or eggplant. Serves 10-12.

EGG AND LEMON SAUCE
"Avgolemono Sauce"

This sauce made from eggs and lemon juice is used as a finishing touch to many Greek recipes, including soups, meat dishes and vegetables.

The recipe given below is for a tart sauce, in which the juice of two lemons is used. If the cook desires a less tart sauce, the lemons may be cut down to one.

The secret in preparing the sauce so it will not curdle is to pour hot broth from the main dish into the eggs while they are being beaten. This procedure heats the eggs to the same temperature and eliminates curdling.

  4 eggs Juice of 2 lemons 3 tbsp. water
  Broth from food in which it is to be used.

Beat eggs and water until light and fluffy, beating constantly, then add hot broth gradually, continuing the beating. When eggs are light and foamy, pour in lemon juice. Stir well, and pour immediately over food. Allow to settle several minutes before serving.

CREAM SAUCE NO. 1
"Krema"

1 quart milk	3 heaping tbsp. flour
1 stick butter (½ cup)	4 eggs well beaten
Salt	

Heat half of milk in large saucepan over medium flame for 7 minutes. Into remaining milk gradually sift in flour and stir until mixture is smooth.

Add eggs and stir vigorously until all is well-blended and smooth. Slowly add to hot milk. Salt to taste and continue cooking for 15 minutes or until mixture thickens and comes to a boil. Remove immediately and stir.

CREAM SAUCE No. 2
"Krema"

½ stick butter (¼ cup)	½ cup grated cheese (Kaseri
2 tbsp. flour	or Kefaloteri)
2 cups milk	4 eggs.
Salt and pepper	

Over medium flame brown flour with butter lightly for about 8-10 minutes, stirring occasionally to avoid scorching. Add milk gradually stirring constantly. Cook 20 minutes, stirring occasionally.

When it begins to bubble remove immediately from flame. Beat eggs well for 5-7 minutes. Add to mixture along with cheese. Mix thoroughly. Season to taste.

SOUP RECIPES

CHICKEN SOUP WITH AVGOLEMONO SAUCE
"Kota Supa Avgolemono"

½ cup rice (or manestra)   Salt and pepper
1 chicken about 6 lbs.   1 tbsp. butter
3 quarts water

Sauce Ingredients

4 eggs   Juice of two lemons   3 tbsp. water

Clean and wash fowl thoroughly and place in large saucepan with water. Bring to a boil over high flame. Reduce heat to medium and cook 1 hour or until tender. Remove fowl from broth, salt and pepper to taste. May be lightly browned in oven if desired.

Add rice to broth, salt and pepper to taste and if broth

is thin, add butter. Cook for 20 minutes. Remove from flame and prepare Avgolemono sauce. Pour over remaining broth, mix well and serve hot. Serves 7-8.

FISH SOUP WITH AVGOLEMONO SAUCE
"Psari Supa"

1 whole trout, 2 lbs.	2 carrots sliced thin
3 qt. water	½ green pepper chopped
3 celery stalks (leaves included) chopped	½ cup rice (long grain)
	Salt and pepper
⅔ cup olive oil	

Clean and wash fish well; cut into 3-inch pieces. Salt and pepper well. Clean and wash all vegetables and place in large saucepan with olive oil and water. Boil over high flame for 10 minutes. Reduce heat and continue boiling over medium flame for 40 minutes. Add fish and cook for 20 minutes. Transfer fish with spatula to avoid breaking, onto large platter and keep warm until time to serve.

Strain broth through fine sieve into another pan. Mash vegetables through sieve into broth. Place back on stove and bring to boiling point. Add rice, and salt and pepper to taste.

Reduce heat to medium; cook 20 minutes or until rice is tender. Remove from fire. Prepare avgolemono sauce, using 4 eggs, 2 lemons, and 4 tbsp. water. Pour avgolemono sauce into broth, stir well. Serve very hot. Serves 7-8.

GREEK EASTER SOUP
"Mageritsa"

2-3 lbs. haslets (lung and heart only—omit spleen and liver)	4 large scallions chopped fine
¾ cup butter (1½ sticks)	1 bunch anitho chopped fine
3½ quarts water	Salt and pepper.

Wash haslets thoroughly and boil in 2 qts. water over

medium heat for 25 minutes. As it begins to boil, remove scum which forms on top, continuing to do this until broth is clear.

Remove meat and cool, then chop fine until it is the size of rice grains. Place in large saucepan and add butter, anitho, scallions, and saute until all excess water is absorbed for about 15 minutes.

Strain broth and measure, adding water to make 3½ quarts. Salt and pepper to taste, and add meat ingredients. Bring to a boil and cook over medium heat for 1 hour.

Remove from heat and prepare avgolemono sauce (page 2), pouring over soup. Stir well and serve very hot.

Note: Ingredients for avgolemono—6 eggs, ¾ cup juice and 2 tbsp. water.

Serves 8-10.

WHITE BEAN SOUP
"Fasolya Soupa"

1½ lbs. white beans	2 carrots sliced
1 cup olive oil	3 celery stalks chopped
2 onions chopped fine	½ can tomatoes
2 garlic buds	Salt and pepper

Soak beans in saucepan of water for five hours. Drain and cover with cold water. Bring to a boil and add remainder of ingredients.

Continue boiling for approximately 45 minutes, or until beans are done. Season to taste. Serves 4-5.

LENTIL SOUP
"Faki Yiahni"

½ lb. lentils	2 garlic cloves chopped fine
1 No. 2 can tomatoes	6 cups hot water
2 onions chopped fine	Salt and pepper

Clean and wash lentils. Place in large pot and add all

ingredients. Salt and pepper to taste. Cover and bring to a boiling point over high flame. Reduce heat and cook for 1½ hours. Serve as for soup with a little dash of vinegar if desired. Serves 4-5.

GREEK BEAN SOUP
"Fasolotha"

½ lb. Greek beans	1 large onion chopped fine
¾ cup pure olive oil	2 carrots sliced thin
1 No. 2 can tomatoes	2 quarts water
4 celery stalks chopped, leaves included	Salt and pepper

Soak beans overnight and drain off water in the morning. In a large saucepan, bring beans to boil in water over high flame. Reduce heat and cook for 1½ hours.

Then add remaining ingredients and salt and pepper to taste. Bring to a boil quickly then reduce heat again and continue cooking for 2 hours or until beans are tender. Serve hot. Serves 4-5.

CHEESES

THE Greek people, like all other Europeans use cheese for seasoning many foods, in addition to serving them as appetizers and along with certain meals.

Perhaps the most popular cheese is the Greek Feta cheese, which is a milky white cheese, and comes packed in a wooden bucket or in large wooden barrels to retain its flavor. This particular cheese is a product made from goats' milk, and is found in every Greek home. It is used in salads and as a food to be served with crackers or crisp Greek bread.

Next in popularity is the Kefaloteri, which is a hard cheese used in preparing meat and vegetable dinners. It is a favorite in the preparation of spaghetti or macaroni.

Kaseri is a firm white cheese, mildly flavored and used for slicing, as is the Greek Provolone cheese.

Also used in spaghetti menus, however not as popular, is the Ricotta or Mezethra cheese; a hard, easy to grate cheese.

CHEESE AND MILK RECIPES

GREEK CLABBER
"Yaourti"

1 quart milk   ¼ cup yeast

Over a medium flame bring milk to a boil, stirring occasionally. Then boil constantly for 20 minutes, stirring to keep milk from forming scum. Cool to lukewarm temperature.

Pour off ½ cup of milk into prepared yeast and stir well. Pour this mixture into remaining milk and mix well.

Cover the milk with a cloth then place lid over cloth. Allow to stand overnight or approximately 11 hours. At this point Yaourti has thickened.

Pour Yaourti into a cheesecloth bag, which is suspended over a deep saucepan. Allow liquid to drip from bag for about 8 hours, or until all liquid has been removed.

Remove Yaourti from bag and beat with a rotary beater for 2 minutes. Serve with dolmathes, pilafe or in individual custard cups. Serves 4.

This is one of the favorites of the Greek people, and is

considered a hearty food when partaken with thick slices of Greek bread. It is known also for its curative powers, when eaten by those suffering from stomach ailments. It may be kept in a covered jar in the refrigerator for many days, and retain its flavor.

YEAST FOR YAOURTI
"Mayia"

½ cup warm milk   1 tsp. lemon juice

Add strained lemon juice to the milk, stir once then cover with a cloth and set aside in a warm place. Avoid moving cup and allow to stand for 24 hours.

At the end of this time, take another cup, into which pour ½ cup milk. To this add 1½ tbsp. from the first cup of milk. Cover and allow this to stand 24 hours. The next day, into another ½ cup of milk, add 1½ tbsp. from the second making, cover and let stand for 24 hours also. This process is repeated for seven days, then at the end of that time, the last yeast mixture is ready to use in preparing yaourti.

This recipe is given for those who do not have yaourti already on hand or cannot borrow a bit from a neighbor. It is usually kept in the home from each making, in order that it may be used when needed. Approximately ½ cup from a making of yaourti is sufficient to use as yeast in preparing a new batch of yaourti.

BAKED CHEESE PUDDING
"Tiropeta"

1½ doz. eggs	½ cup cream or milk
1 lb. cottage cheese	2 tbsp. sifted flour
1 lb. Feta cheese	½ lb. butter.
½ lb. pastry sheets (filo)	

Beat eggs slightly, mix cheeses and add to eggs, blending thoroughly. Mix flour and milk and add to eggs.

Grease a pan 10 x 15 with butter and place 4 pastry sheets in bottom, brushing each sheet with melted butter. Pour in cheese mixture and top with remaining sheets, brushing in between each one with butter. Brush top with remaining butter and bake for one hour in oven 350°. Cool before cutting in squares. Serves 10.

BAKED CHEESE PIE
"Tiropita"

2 pounds pastry sheets (filo) 2 cups butter melted
6 eggs   2 tsp. salt.
2 cups feta cheese

In a greased pan 9 x 13 place half the pastry sheets. Beat eggs until fluffy, add cheese and salt and mix well. Spread over pastry sheets, and top with remainder of pastry.

Brush the top with melted butter and bake in a moderate oven for 45 minutes. Allow to cool before serving. Cut in squares. Serves 6-8.

FETA CHEESE PUDDING
"Tiropeta"

1½ lbs. feta cheese   ¼ cup rice
6 eggs   ¼ cup heavy cream
1½ lbs butter melted   1 lb. pastry sheets

Cook rice in water until done, drain and set aside. Beat eggs until light and fluffy. Mix cheese with cream and add to eggs, continue beating until completely dissolved, then add rice.

Grease a pan 10 x 15 with melted butter and place half the pastry sheets in the pan, brushing each sheet with butter. Pour in cheese mixture and top with remainder of sheets, brushing each layer with butter also. Brush top with butter and bake in oven 350° for 45 minutes. Serve cool. Serves 10.

CREAM CHEESE
"Krema Tiri"

Pour 2½ pints of milk into a heavy crock and keep in a warm place until sour.

When it thickens, pour into a piece of muslin then gather ends and hang over a bowl, until all liquid drains out. This process will take approximately 12 hours.

Pour remaining cheese into a bowl. May be served with cream. Serves 4.

Epiphany Day

THROUGHOUT the Christian world, wherever there is a Greek Orthodox church, the celebration of Epiphany Day takes place on January 6th.

This day, which commemorates the baptism of Jesus in the river Jordan is appropriately celebrated everywhere, however, it is in Tarpon Springs, Florida; where a large Greek colony is located, that the ancient customs are observed.

Annually thousands of people come from all parts of the world to witness the ceremony of the "diving for the cross", which has led the celebration to be commonly called Greek Cross Day.

It is at this time that high dignitaries of the Greek Orthodox Church gather at this little community to participate in the rituals at St. Nicholas Greek Orthodox Church. Patriarch Athenegoras, now head of the Greek Orthodox Church, has often been the chief celebrant at these occasions.

Following a long ceremony at the church, the ritual is

climaxed as a procession forms at the church, marches through the streets and ends at Spring Bayou, where hundreds of young Greek boys are awaiting the opportunity to dive for the cross. As they anxiously await the sign from the chief celebrant, the air is tense throughout the thousands who have lined the banks to watch the ceremony. As the scripture is read, a white dove is released to fly over the heads of the crowd. In a moment the priest throws a golden cross into the churning waters, as the boys struggle to reach it. One boy will emerge victorious and to him will go the blessings of the church for the year, as he kneels before the priest.

This is one of the most beautiful ceremonies to be seen in the United States.

SALAD RECIPES

GREEK SALAD

A beautiful sight to see, in addition to being delightful to eat, is a colorful Greek salad tastefully arranged on a large platter built up into a peak at the center until it resembles a resplendent Christmas tree, shiny and green.

The secret of the salad lies in the arranging of the many ingredients, and in the deft handling of the seasoning. Large lettuce leaves are first placed on the platter, then the remainder of the lettuce is shredded and piled into a mound in the center of platter. Upon this mound are added the other vegetables, one here, one there, until the completed salad is ready to serve.

Stories have been written about the Greek Salads, and in many parts of the country these salads have become famous. Above all, proper seasoning is the making of the salad.

½ head lettuce shredded
3 celery stalks chopped fine, leaves included
1 medium cucumber sliced
2 medium tomatoes sliced lengthwise
½ green pepper sliced
4 Greek anchovies
Origano salt and pepper
⅓ cup pure olive oil
1 small onion sliced thin
8 Greek olives
4 slices feta cheese
½ avocado sliced
Juice of 1 lemon or 2 tbsp. vinegar

Wash anchovies thoroughly. Wash and clean vegetables. Arrange vegetables on large platter as follows: lettuce, celery, cucumbers, tomatoes, onions, green peppers, avocado. Decorate with anchovies, olives and white cheese. Sprinkle olive oil, lemon juice or vinegar, salt and pepper and origano. Serves 4-5.

MIXED GREEK SALAD

"Salata"

½ head lettuce
3 celery stalks chopped, leaves included
1 medium-sized cucumber
1 small onion sliced thin
2 medium tomatoes sliced thin
⅓ cup pure olive oil
½ green pepper chopped
8 black olives
4 pieces feta cheese
4 salted sardines
1 tsp. origano
3 tbsp. vinegar (or juice of 2 lemons)

Wash and clean all vegetables thoroughly. Cut lettuce into 1-inch pieces, and cut all other vegetables into bowl. Wash sardines to remove all salt and use on top of salad.

Mix all ingredients well, add seasonings and toss until thoroughly covered with seasonings. Sprinkle with origano and serve immediately. **Serves 4-5.**

SPINACH SALAD
"Spanaki Salata"

4 lbs. spinach
⅓ cup pure olive oil
Juice of 2 lemons (¼ cup)
Salt and pepper

Clean and wash spinach thoroughly. Boil in 1 quart of water for 15 minutes until tender. Drain well and place in salad bowl.

Add olive oil and lemon juice and salt and pepper to taste. Mix thoroughly. Serve cold or hot. Serves 4-5.

GREEK HOT POTATO SALAD
"Patato Salata"

8 potatoes
1 large onion
Salt and pepper
⅓ cup olive oil
Juice of 1 lemon
Origano

Boil potatoes until almost tender, remove from water and peal. Slice in quarters and then in halves. Chop onion fine and add to potatoes. Place in a large bowl and cover with olive oil, lemon juice, salt and pepper to taste. Sprinkle with origano. Toss lightly and serve warm.

Seasoning the potatoes while warm is part of the trick for higher flavor, as the hot potatoes absorb the seasoning thoroughly. Serves 6.

LIMA BEAN SALAD
"Fasolya Salata"

2 cups lima beans
1 large onion
Salt and pepper
⅓ cup olive oil
Juice of 1 lemon

Cook lima beans until tender. Drain and place in a large bowl. Chop one large onion and add to beans. Salt and pepper to taste and add olive oil and lemon juice. Toss lightly and serve while warm.

More lemon juice may be added if desired. Serves 4.

VEGETABLE SALAD GREEK STYLE

"Salata"

½ head cabbage shredded	1 doz. olives (black)
½ lb. string beans cooked until tender	4 large beets cooked sliced
	4 tbsp. vinegar
1 tbsp. capers	1 tsp. mustard
6 tbsp. olive oil	Salt and pepper

Mix cabbage, beans, capers, olives and beets in a large bowl. Salt and pepper to taste. Pour over dressing made of vinegar, olive oil and mustard. Serves 6.

GREEK SALAD DRESSING

1 cup vinegar	1 tsp. sugar
2 cups olive oil	2 garlic cloves chopped fine
1 tsp. Worcestershire Sauce	1 tsp. origano
Salt and pepper to taste	

Mix all ingredients in a large jar. Cover and shake well. Let stand for two days at room temperature.

Use to sprinkle over vegetable salads, always shaking well before using.

VEGETABLE RECIPES

In the following vegetable recipes, it will be noted that tomatoes and tomato paste are also used extensively for flavoring, as they are in meats.

Olive oil and butter are used in browning the vegetables before they are cooked in many of the recipes and for seasoning in others.

Many of the vegetables are prepared to be the main dish at a Greek table, supplemented with a bit of salad or cheese as a side dish.

A vegetable dish prepared by a Greek recipe is an adventure worth trying.

SPINACH PIE
"Spanakopita"

"The lowly spinach here takes on the guise of a delectable well-browned pie, made with thin layers of Greek pastry, properly combined with ingredients, which make it one of the specialties in the Greek homes; to be served on special occasions, particularly when company calls for dinner."

2 lbs. spinach	3 tbsp. olive oil for topping
10 pastry sheets	2 cups chopped feta cheese
1 medium onion chopped fine	7 eggs
3 tbsp. butter	½ cup olive oil
Salt and pepper	

Clean and wash spinach thoroughly. Cut into 2-inch pieces. Drain, place in bowl, and rub 1 tbsp. salt into spinach leaves with hands until it is all well covered. Let stand 15 minutes. Drain well for 30 minutes.

Brown onion lightly in hot olive oil. Beat eggs well and add eggs, cheese and onion to spinach in large bowl. Salt and pepper to taste. Mix olive oil and butter and brush a 9 x 13 pan lightly. Place 5 pastry sheets into pan, brushing each sheet with butter. Spread spinach mixture, then place 5 additional sheets on top. With sharp knife, cut through the top 5 sheets in three places.

Bake in oven 375° for 50 minutes. Cut into squares and serve hot. Serves 15.

SPINACH AND RICE

"Spanaki me Rize"

2 lbs. spinach	1½ cups rice (long grain)
2 med. onions chopped fine	⅓ cup butter (½ stick)
3 cups boiling water	Salt and pepper

Clean and wash spinach thoroughly, cut in halves. Saute onion in olive oil in saucepan, until soft and tender. Add spinach. Cover and cook about 10 minutes over medium flame until soft but not tender.

Vegetable Recipes 21

Wash rice in cold water several times. Place in bowl with salt and hot water. Soak for 30 minutes. Drain well. Roll in dish towel, and let stand for 20 minutes. Place rice in skillet and add butter and fry for 10 minutes, stirring constantly. Pour off liquid from spinach, and add water to make 2 parts water and one part rice.

Place back on high flame, bring to boil and add rice. Stir and cover and immediately reduce heat to cook 10 minutes on low. Do not remove cover during cooking process, however to avoid scorching, grasp saucepan with both hands and twist several times from side to side occasionally.

Remove from fire and stir well. Allow to set for 10 minutes before serving. Serves 5-6.

SPINACH TURNOVERS HALKI STYLE
"Halkitikes Spanakopites"

2 lbs. spinach	3 cups self-rising flour
1 large onion chopped fine	1 cup water
1½ cups olive oil	Salt and pepper

Clean and wash spinach thoroughly. Boil for 5 minutes, drain and cut as you would for salad. Saute onion in ½ cup olive oil for 5 minutes, add spinach, salt and pepper and cover, cooking for 12 minutes. Stir occasionally. Remove cover during last 3 minutes of cooking. Allow to cool.

In a large bowl mix flour, ⅓ cup olive oil and water and knead until well blended. Moisten hands with olive oil and pinch off a small portion of the dough. Roll out on a board which has been moistened with olive oil, until ¼ inch in thickness and from 3 to 4 inches in diameter. Place 2 tbsp. of the spinach mixture in center and fold pastry over to form a semi-circle. Press edges together with finger-tips. Fry quickly in ½ cup olive oil over medium flame until golden brown on both sides.

Place in a bowl, cover and allow to stand 10 minutes before serving. May be served warm or cold. Serves 6-8.

BAKED SQUASH AND CHEESE
"Kolokethya me Tiri"

2 cups grated cheese (kefaloteri)	3 eggs
4 large squash (yellow)	Olive oil for frying

Wash squashes and slice in pieces about one inch in thickness. Brown in olive oil, and arrange in a greased baking dish.

Beat eggs until light and fluffy and add grated cheese. Pour one tsp. of eggs on each squash, then bake in oven 350° for 15 minutes. Serve hot. Serves 5-6.

SQUASH CASSEROLE
"Kolokethya Pita"

½ lb. pastry sheets	¼ cup olive oil
3 lbs. squash (white)	1 tbsp. shortening
3 onions chopped fine	½ cup rice
10 eggs.	½ lb. grated cheese (kefaloteri)

Brown onions in shortening, add ½ cup water and cook until tender over medium flame. Add rice and sufficient water to cook rice until tender. Cut squash into small pieces and add to rice, cook for three minutes, then remove from stove and allow to cool. Beat eggs until fluffy, add cheese and mix with squash mixture.

In a pan 10 x 12 place four pastry sheets, brushing in between each one with melted shortening, pour in squash mixture and place remaining pastry sheets over this, brushing with shortening also.

Bake in oven 350° for 20 minutes, then reduce heat to 325° and bake until golden brown. Serves 6-8.

ISLAND STYLE SQUASH
"Kolekethya Giahni"

1 lb. small Greek squash	2 onions chopped fine
½ cup olive oil	1 tbsp. chopped parsley
1½ cup tomatoes	Salt and pepper

Brown onion lightly in olive oil over medium flame, then add tomatoes, parsley and sufficient water to cover. Slice squash into small pieces and add to water. Cover and cook for approximately 40 minutes over medium flame until done. Serves 4-5.

SQUASH PATTIES
"Kolekethya Keftedes"

1½ lbs. squash (white)	1 cup cracker-meal
1 onion chopped fine	1 tbsp. parsley chopped fine
2 eggs	3 tbsp. grated cheese
Olive oil	Salt and pepper

Scrape outside of squash to remove tough outer skin. Grate remainder with coarse grater into large bowl. Salt and let stand for ½ hour. Drain water and add parsley, cracker-meal, cheese, eggs, onion, salt and pepper. Form into small cakes and roll in flour. Fry in hot olive oil until golden brown. Serve hot. Serves 4-5.

SQUASH GREEK STYLE
"Kolokethya me Saltsa"

6 white squash	Salt and pepper
1 tbsp. vinegar	1 cup water
2 tbsp. flour	Olive oil for frying

Slice squash in thin round slices and fry until brown in olive oil. Set aside while preparing gravy in olive oil by browning flour, add salt and pepper, water and vinegar.

When it begins to thicken add squash. Cover and let simmer for 30 minutes over medium flame. Add more water if it cooks down. Serve hot. Serves 4.

STRING BEANS GRECIAN STYLE

"Fresca Fasolya Giahni"

3 lbs. string beans	2 large potatoes sliced quarters
5 scallions chopped	3 tbsp. parsley chopped fine
1 cup of water	½ cup tomatoes
1 green pepper chopped	2 tbsp. butter
2 large carrots sliced thin	Salt and pepper
2 tbsp. olive oil	

Clean and cut string beans in half. Wash and drain. Place all vegetables in medium saucepan. Top with parsley. Add butter, oil and one cup water, salt and pepper to taste. Cover and cook over high flame until the boiling point is reached. Lower flame to medium and continue cooking for 45 minutes until vegetables are tender. Serves 4-5.

STRING BEANS HALKI STYLE

"Fresca Fasolia me Lathe"

2 lbs. string beans	3 onions chopped fine
1 cup olive oil	1 tbsp. parsley chopped fine
1 cup tomatoes	Salt and pepper
1 cup water	

String beans and cut into 1-inch pieces. Brown onions in olive oil, add tomatoes, water and parsley. Season to taste and bring to a boil. Add string beans and cook over moderate heat for one hour. Serves 4-5.

Vegetable Recipes

STUFFED PEPPERS SYMRNA STYLE

"Gemistes Peperies"

10 medium-sized peppers	½ bunch parsley chopped fine
1 lb. hamburg	1 onion chopped fine
½ cup boiled, drained rice	1 garlic clove chopped fine
3 eggs well-beaten	½ cup water
1 No. 2 can tomatoes	Salt and pepper

Wash peppers, remove stems and seeds. Combine all other ingredients except tomatoes, and mix thoroughly. Stuff peppers, and arrange in baking pan. Add tomatoes and 1 cup water. Bake in medium oven for 1 hour or until peppers are done. Serves 5-6.

STUFFED PEPPERS

"Gemistes Peperies"

14 medium-sized peppers	1 cup rice (long grain)
1½ lbs. lean hamburger	½ cup butter (1 stick)
3 medium onions chopped fine	1 tsp. cinnamon
1 No. 2 can tomatoes	1½ cups water
1 tbsp. mint leaf chopped fine	Salt and pepper

Wash peppers and cut stems carefully, saving tops for covers. Saute hamburger in skillet for 5 minutes stirring occasionally. Add butter and onions and brown for 5 minutes. Add rice and fry for 10 minutes stirring constantly.

Add tomatoes, cinnamon, salt and pepper to taste and cook about 2 minutes more. Stuff peppers and replace tops to keep stuffing in place. Place in baking pan, add water and bake for 1 hour and 20 minutes in oven 475°.

Baste peppers occasionally with pan juice. Serve very hot. Serves 7-8.

STUFFED PEPPERS HALKI STYLE

"Gemistes Peperies"

2 lbs. hamburger	2 large onions chopped fine
⅔ cup rice (long grain)	2 tbsp. thiosmo (mint leaf)
1 No. 2 can tomatoes	⅔ cup butter
1½ cups water	15 large peppers

Salt and pepper

Mix all ingredients well and salt and pepper to taste. Cut tops off peppers, and fill with mixture. Replace tops and arrange closely in a large pan, add water and bake in oven 450° for 1 hour and 15 minutes. Serves 8.

GALAXIDI STUFFED TOMATOES

"Domates Yemestes"

12 medium-sized tomatoes	1 tsp. parsley chopped fine
1 lb. hamburger	2 onions chopped fine
½ cup rice	Pulp from tomatoes
½ stick butter	1 egg
1 cup water	Cinnamon (about 1 tsp.)

Cut tops off tomatoes, allowing a hinge so they may be raised up and down. Scoop out pulp with teaspoon. Add water pulp and bring to a boil, to be used later.

Mix hamburger, rice, onion, parsley, egg, cinnamon, salt and pepper to taste. Pour tomato pulp through sieve, and add juice to meat mixture, enough to make it thinner. Fill each tomato with mixture and top with a slice of butter. Turn upside down in deep baking dish. Arrange the tomatoes close together so they will cook better. Pour remainder of tomato juice over them. Cook in oven 375° for 1 hour until done. Serves 4-5.

STUFFED TOMATOES AND EGGPLANTS
"Gemistes Domates me Melzana"

1 lb. grated cheese (kefaloteri)	2 tbsp. butter
10 firm tomatoes	3 eggs
4 small eggplants	Salt and pepper

Wash tomatoes thoroughly, then cut off tops, allowing tops to remain hinged on with a part of the skin. Scoop out pulp and set aside.

Bake the eggplants in an uncovered dish for an hour, then remove and peel carefully. Mash pulp until creamy, add cheese, eggs, pepper and butter.

Fill the hollow tomatoes with the eggplant mixture, placing a dab of butter on top of each. Close lids over mixture and place in a baking dish and bake in oven 350° until tomatoes begin to brown and shrivel. Serves 5.

STUFFED CABBAGE LEAVES
"Lahana Dolmades"

1 medium head cabbage	1 cup long grain rice
1 lb. hamburger	1 egg
2 small onions chopped fine	½ tsp. cinnamon
½ cup butter	Hot water
Salt and pepper	

Cook cabbage until slightly tender. Remove from water and peel off leaves, allowing them to cool, for easier handling. Trim off the outer stems, and prepare the following mixture.

Mix thoroughly, eggs, hamburger, salt, pepper, onions, half of butter, rice, cinnamon and add enough hot water to make the mixture easy to handle.

Place a tablespoonful in center of each cabbage leaf, folding edges over, until a compact roll is made. Arrange close together in medium saucepan, and cut up remaining butter over the top layer. Add 1 cup water. Place a dish over the rolls, so they will not break in cooking. Cover and cook for 35 minutes, until rice is tender.

Pour off gravy, and make avgolemono sauce, using 1 egg and juice of ½ lemon. Pour over rolls and allow to stand several minutes before serving. This enhances the flavor of the dish. Serves 4-5.

STUFFED GRAPEVINE LEAVES
"Dolmathes"

This tasty dish is one of the most famous of Greek foods, served on special occasions, such as baptisms, receptions and for "special guest" dinners. The meal is so complete with vegetables, meat and starch, that only a leafy salad is required to be served along with it. The making of the dish is the tart avgolemono sauce which is poured over the rolls when it is cooked. The sauce may be made more tart or less tart by the increasing or decreasing of the lemon juice.

- 1 lb. ground beef
- 1 15-oz. jar grapevine leaves (cabbage leaves may be substituted by boiling head of cabbage until tender, and removing each leaf, trimming stem)
- ½ cup butter (measure then melt)
- 1 cup canned tomatoes, pulp and juice
- 1½ cups hot water
- 2 medium onions chopped fine
- ½ cup rice (long grain)
- 2 tbsp. mint leaf or parsley chopped fine
- Salt and pepper

Mix all ingredients except leaves and water. Salt and pepper to taste. In the center of each leaf, place a heaping teaspoon of mixture. Starting from stem, roll, turning in ends and roll tightly to avoid filling from coming out. Form into oblong rolls.

Arrange in compact layers in large saucepan, and place a dish over the rolls, to prevent breaking up when boiling. Add water. Bring to boil over high flame. Reduce heat and cook 25 minutes over medium heat. Remove from stove and drain off broth into a separate bowl, to be used in avgolemono sauce (page 2). Pour over rolls and let stand. Serve hot. Serves 5-6.

GRAPEVINE LEAVES WITH SQUASH FILLING
"Kolokithya Dolmathes"

1 lb. small yellow squash chopped fine	1 cup water
2 medium onions	⅓ cup rice (long grain)
1 15-oz. jar grape leaves	½ cup pure olive oil
2 tbsp. mint leaf (*thiosmo*) chopped fine	¾ cup canned tomatoes
	Juice of 1 lemon
	Salt and pepper

Using large bowl, mix squash, onions, mint leaf, rice, olive oil, tomatoes, half of lemon juice, salt and pepper to taste.

Separate grape leaves, and place 1 teaspoon of mixture in center of each leaf. Starting at end of stem, roll into oblong rolls, turning in ends so filling will not come out. Arrange in small saucepan. Pour remaining mixture juice over rolls and add water. Place a dish over rolls so they will not come apart while cooking. Cover and bring to a boil over high flame. Reduce heat and cook 20 minutes. Serve hot. Serves 5-6.

Note: This recipe is a meatless variation of the famous Dolmathe recipe, and is used particularly during Lent, when meats are forbidden in Greek meals.

GRAPEVINE LEAVES WITH RICE FILLING
"Nistisimes Dolmades"

1 jar grape leaves, 15-oz.	3 large onions chopped fine
1 cup rice	2 tbsp. tomato paste
1 cup olive oil	2 tbsp. parsley chopped fine
⅓ cup lemon juice	(or mint leaf)
5 cups water	Salt and pepper

Soak rice for 30 minutes in 2 cups cold water and 1 teaspoon salt. Drain. Saute onion over medium flame with one cup water until tender, for 15 minutes. Add oil and cook 5 minutes. Add rice and tomato paste, salt and pepper to taste. Cook for 5 minutes, stirring occasionally.

Add parsley and cook 3 minutes. Add half of lemon juice and continue cooking for 5 minutes. Spread out grape leaves and place 1 teaspoon of filling in center of each one.

Starting from stem of grape leaf, roll, turn in ends and roll tightly. Arrange in layers in medium compact saucepan. Pour remaining lemon juice over rolls along with 1 cup water.

Cover and bring to a boil for 5 minutes over high flame. Reduce heat to medium and cook 15 minutes. Add 1 more cup of water if the first water added has been absorbed. Reduce heat to low, and continue cooking for 15 minutes or until rice is tender. Serve either hot or cold. Serves 4-5.

SPAGHETTI WITH BUTTER
"Spaghetti me Tsigaristo Vootiro"

1 lb. spaghetti ½ stick butter (¼ cup)
1 cup grated cheese (Kaseri or Kefaloteri) Salt to taste

Cook spaghetti for 10 minutes in 3 parts of boiling water, which has been salted.

Vegetable Recipes 31

Drain thoroughly. Brown butter slightly in saucepan over high flame. Pour over spaghetti. Mix thoroughly. Sprinkle generously with grated cheese. Serves 5-6.

This is a basic recipe for spaghetti to be used with various sauces given elsewhere in the book.

BAKED MACARONI
"Pastitsio"

Part No. 1

2 lbs. lean hamburger	1 tsp. cinnamon
¼ cup butter	2 eggs well beaten
1 can tomato paste, 6-oz.	2 cups boiling water
2 large onions chopped fine	Salt and pepper

Blend tomato paste with 1 cup water. Saute hamburger over high flame for 15 minutes. Add butter and onions and continue to brown for 15 minutes, stirring occasionally. Add tomato paste, cinnamon, 1 cup water, salt and pepper to taste. Cover and cook for 15 minutes over medium flame. Remove cover and cook for 10 minutes or until it thickens. Stir occasionally. Remove from flame and cool. Add eggs and mix well.

Part No. 2

1½ lbs. thin macaroni	2 eggs well beaten
½ cup butter	1 cup grated cheese
Salt to taste	(Kafaloteri)

Cook macaroni in rapidly boiling water which has been salted, for 10 minutes. Drain well in collander. Put half of macaroni in bowl, add eggs and mix thoroughly. Arrange in bottom of baking pan 11 x 14. Sprinkle generously with half of grated cheese. Spread and pat firmly meat sauce over this. Arrange remaining macaroni over hamburger sauce and again sprinkle with remaining cheese. Melt butter and pour over entire mixture. Top with Krema Sauce No. 1 (page 3).

Sprinkle lightly with grated cheese and cinnamon. Bake in oven 400° for 30 minutes. Cool for 15 minutes before serving. Cut into squares and serve. Serves 16.

Note: This recipe will brown very easily in oven, therefore it is advisable to watch it carefully during baking process.

LENTILS WITH EGG NOODLES

"Kouloorea"

This is a favorite dish of the island of Halki, in the Dodecanese Island group of Greece. A great many natives use rise in place of the noodles, which makes the dish equally as tasty.

1 lb. lentils	1 12-oz. bag noodles
2 quarts water	1 large onion chopped fine
1 cup water	1 cup olive oil
1 No. 2 can tomatoes	Salt and pepper to taste

Place lentils in large saucepan with 2 quarts of water. Cover and bring to a boil over high flame. Reduce flame to medium and cook for one hour. Add noodles and 1 cup water. Season with salt and pepper to taste.

Cover and continue cooking for 25 minutes or until noodles are tender, stirring occasionally. Remove from stove. Brown onion lightly for 6 or 7 minutes. Pour into lentil mixture, stir well and serve hot. Serves 8-9.

BAKED GARBANZOS

"Revithya Psita"

2 No. 2 cans garbanzos
1 large onion chopped fine
2 garlic cloves chopped fine
1 tsp. lendrolivano

2 large very ripe tomatoes
1 tbsp. tomato paste
¾ cup olive oil
Salt and pepper

Place garbanzos in baking pan and arrange remaining ingredients over same. Salt and pepper to taste. Bake in oven 475° for 40 minutes. Serves 5-6.

GARBANZOS AND RICE

"Revithya me Rize"

1 No. 2 can garbanzo beans
1 cup rice
2 cups hot water

1 large onion
½ cup olive oil

"This meatless dish is one of the favorites of the Greek people during the Lenten season. Served as a main dish, with an added salad, it becomes a nourishing meal in itself. Care should be taken in twisting the saucepan from side to side during the cooking process in order that the ingredients will not scorch. Removing the lid and stirring, robs the dish of its flavor."

Saute onion until soft and golden brown in olive oil for 5 minutes. Add beans and continue cooking for 5 minutes. Add water and cook on high flame for a few minutes. Add rice and reduce heat immediately to low.

Cover and cook for 10 minutes. Do not uncover until time is up, but turn saucepan slowly from side to side several times.

Heat ⅓ cup olive oil and pour over top of rice and

beans. Cover and allow to stand for several minutes before serving. Serves 4-5.

BAKED RICE GREEK STYLE

"Pilaffe tou Fournou"

2 cups long grain rice   4⅓ cups chicken or meat broth
5 cups boiling water   1 tbsp. salt

Wash rice thoroughly and soak in boiling salted water for half an hour. Strain and wash rice thoroughly then place in bowl.

Pour broth into small baking pan and bring to a boil over direct heat. In the meantime heat oven to 550°. Pour rice into broth, stir well, cover and place baking pan into oven. Turn off oven heat and allow rice to cook on receding heat for 10-15 minutes. Do not uncover while baking.

Remove from oven, stir well, cover with a clean dish towel. Replace cover and allow to stand 20-25 minutes before serving.

This rice dish is excellent served with "yaourti."

If rice is to be used with chicken dish, use chicken broth. If with meat, use meat broth. Serves 6.

PILAFFE GREEK STYLE

"Pilaffe"

2 cups rice   2 tbsp. canned tomatoes
1 stick butter   Salt and pepper
4 cups meat stock

Melt butter in skillet and brown rice for 5 to 8 minutes. Gradually add hot meat stock and allow to simmer for 10 minutes, with cover on. Add tomatoes salt and pepper and cook until rice is done. All liquid should be absorbed by the rice when it is well done.

Allow to stand 15 minutes covered before serving. Serve hot. Serve 4.

BAKED GREEN VEGETABLES
"Lahanika Psita"

3 medium-size green squash
1 medium-size onion sliced
5 scallions chopped fine
4 tbsp. parsley chopped fine
¾ cup toast crumbs
2 tbsp. butter
3 small carots sliced ¼ inch

1 green pepper sliced fine
½ cup fresh peas
2 potatoes sliced
1 cup canned tomatoes
2 tbsp. olive oil
Salt and pepper

Wash and scrape squash lightly, slice in ½-inch pieces, salt and let stand 10 minutes. Arrange all vegetables in baking pan 12 x 7 as listed in layers, except bread crumbs, oil and butter.

Salt and pepper to taste. Sprinkle top with bread crumbs, add oil and butter, cover and bake in oven 350° for 1½ hours or until all vegetables are tender. Baste occasionally. Uncover for last 15 minutes and continue baking. Serves 4-5.

POTATO PANCAKES
"Patata Keftedes"

4 large potatoes
½ cup grated cheese
1 heaping tbsp. butter
2 eggs well beaten

½ cup flour
¾ cups olive oil
Salt and pepper

Boil and mash patotoes, add butter and cool. Place in a deep mixing bowl. Stir into this mixture beaten eggs, cheese, salt and pepper.

Mold mixture into cakes about 2½ inches in diameter and ½ inch thick. Pat firmly in flour. Fry in very hot olive oil about 5 minutes or until golden brown on both sides. Serve hot. Serves 7-8.

BAKED CAULIFLOWER WITH CREAM SAUCE
"Psito Kounoupithi"

1 head of cauliflower about 3 lbs.
1 quart water   Salt to taste
Cream Sauce Recipe No. 2

Wash and break cauliflower into small pieces. Cook in rapidly boiling water which has been salted, for 12-15 minutes or until tender but not soft. Drain and arrange in small baking dish.

Prepare Cream Sauce No. 2 (page 3). Take half of sauce and mix well with cauliflower. Pour remaining sauce over cauliflower. Bake in oven 475° for 25 minutes, in pan 10½ x 8½ inches.

Cool and cut into squares, 3 inches in size. Remove with spatula to avoid breaking. Serve warm. Serves 9.

CARROT LOAF
"Carrota tou Fournou"

4 large carrots grated	½ lb. hamburger
1 celery stalk chopped fine	½ cup canned tomatoes
1 medium onion chopped fine	½ cup butter
1 egg	¾ cup toast crumbs
2 tbsp. light cream	Salt and pepper

Mix carrots, celery, onion, egg, hamburger, tomatoes, crumbs and cream and blend thoroughly. Add butter, salt and pepper to taste. If too dry add 2 tbsp. tomatoes. Mix well. Bake in loaf pan in moderate oven for 30 minutes or until golden brown but not dry. Cut in 3-inch squares and serve hot. Serves 4-5.

ARTICHOKES HALKI STYLE

"Aginares Halki Style"

Juice of 3 lemons
2 chopped onions
Salt and pepper

10 or 12 artichokes
1½ cups olive oil
1 tbsp. flour

Remove outer leaves from artichokes, using only the hearts, cover with water and juice of 2 lemons, for 10 minutes.

Brown onions in olive oil then add flour, browning flour, add salt, pepper and juice from one lemon. Remove artichokes and arrange in baking dish. Pour remainder of ingredients over artichokes, and add sufficient water to cover. Cook over medium flame for approximately one hour until artichokes are tender. Serves 4-5.

FRIED ARTICHOKES

"Aginares Tiginetos"

12 artichokes
2 lemons
1 cup grated cheese
  (kefaloteri)

3 eggs
1½ cup bread crumbs
  toasted

Remove outer leaves of artichokes, and place hearts in a bowl of water in which has been placed the juice of two lemons. Let stand for a few minutes then boil until tender.

Beat eggs until light and fluffy. Dip each artichoke into egg then into bread crumbs, into the egg again and again into the crumbs. Fry in deep fat until golden brown.

Delicious when served with meats and fowl. Serves 5.

ARTICHOKES WITH GREEN FAVA BEANS

"Aginares me Kookya"

¾ cup olive oil
½ cup tomatoes
1 lb. green fava beans
4 artichokes (large)
1 chopped onion

2 tbsp. chopped parsley
½ bunch chopped scallions
Juice of one lemon
Salt and pepper

Remove outer leaves of artichokes and use only hearts. Split lengthwise and soak in cold water, lemon juice and salt, for 10 minutes.

Brown onion in olive oil then add a little water and simmer until tender. Add artichokes, beans and remainder of ingredients. Season with salt and pepper to taste, add 1 teaspoon lemon juice and cook over low flame in covered saucepan 2½ hours until artichokes are tender. Serves hot. Serves 4-5.

BAKED EGGPLANTS

"Yeimistes Melizanes"

3 medium-size eggplants
1½ lbs. hamburger
¾ cup grated cheese
  (kefaloteri)

2 med. onions chopped fine
¾ cup butter (1½ sticks)
Salt and pepper

Cut stems from eggplant and cut in half lengthwise. Scoop out pulp from centers with a spoon, being careful not to break eggplant. Salt shells to taste and let stand 30 minutes.

Place pulp in large bowl, mash with fork and salt to taste. Allow to stand 30 minutes.

Saute hamburger with onion for 10 minutes, add butter and fry for 7 minutes stirring occasionally.

Rinse eggplant shells and place in baking dish. Add pulp to meat mixture and continue frying for 6 minutes. Cool and add grated cheese and salt and pepper to taste. Fill shells with meat mixture and arrange in baking dish. Any meat mixture left over may be arranged around the eggplants.

Prepare sauce No. 2 (page 3) and top each eggplant with sauce. Bake in 350° oven for 1½ hours watching carefully so it will not burn. Remove eggplants with spatula to avoid breaking. Serve hot. Serves 6.

SMALL GREEK EGGPLANTS
"Mampaildi"

3 lbs. very small eggplants	1 head of garlic
1 No. 2 can tomatoes	1 cup water
⅔ cup olive oil (pure)	1 tsp. salt
5 med. onions cut in half and sliced	Pepper to taste

Wash and cut stems of eggplants. Make one slit in each eggplant. Sprinkle with salt and let stand for 30 minutes. Cut garlic cloves in half lengthwise. Insert ½ of garlic clove in each slit of eggplant.

Fry in hot olive oil for 10 minutes until light brown on all sides and soft. Transfer to large saucepan.

In the same skillet in remaining oil, fry onions until brown. Add tomato, salt and pepper to taste and cook for 10 minutes more.

Pour over eggplants, add water, cover and bring to a boil for 3 minutes. Reduce heat and continue cooking for 40 minutes over medium flame. Stir occasionally to avoid burning as eggplants scorch easily. Serve hot. Serves 9-10.

FRIED EGGPLANT
"Melzana Teganiti"

1 large eggplant	½ cup flour
1 cup olive oil	Salt and pepper

Cut eggplant lengthwise into ½-inch pieces. Wash and drain well. Salt to taste and let stand 20 minutes. Roll in flour. Fry in hot olive oil about two minutes or until soft and light brown on each side.

Remove from frying-pan; place on platter, salt and pepper to taste. Serve with garlic sauce or as a side dish with meat. Serves 3-4.

EGGPLANT AND MEAT CASSEROLE
"Mousaka"

1 tbsp. tomato paste	1 tbsp. parsley chopped fine
7 or 8 eggplants, small size	2 eggs
1 lb. hamburger	8 tbsp. bread crumbs
3 onions chopped fine	Salt and pepper
1 cup water	1 stick butter

1 cup grated cheese (kefaloteri)

Saute meat in 1 teaspoon butter for 5 minutes. Add onions, water, tomato paste, parsley, salt and pepper and cook for 25 minutes stirring occasionally. Add crumbs and beaten egg whites, mix well.

Slice eggplant lengthwise and brown in butter until golden brown. Place one layer of eggplants in a buttered pan, then one layer of the meat mixture, another layer of eggplant, and so on until all ingredients are used ending with eggplant layer.

Top with white sauce made as follows:

3 cups **milk**	6 tablespoons butter
7 tablespoons flour	Dash of salt and nutmeg

Boil milk in a saucepan, then melt butter in another

pan, and stir in flour, salt and nutmeg. Slowly pour milk over this and stir until smooth sauce is obtained.

Pour over mousaka, sprinkle with grated cheese and bake in oven 350° for half an hour or until well brown. Serves 4-5.

EGGPLANT CASSEROLE
"Mousaka Calamata Style"

1½ lbs. hamburger	2 eggs well beaten
6 med. onions chopped fine	½ cup grated cheese (kefaloteri)
1 large can tomatoes	
3 medium eggplants	6 tbsp. bread crumbs
2 tbsp. chopped parsley	¼ cup red wine
2 sticks butter	Salt and pepper

Brown the onions and hamburger in half of the butter. Add parsley, tomatoes, wine, salt and pepper to taste and cook on low flame until liquid is absorbed. Set aside to cool, then add eggs, cheese and 3 tablespoons bread crumbs. Mix well, season to taste.

While this is being prepared, slice eggplants lengthwise. Fry each slice in butter, browning on each side.

Sprinkle the bottom of a 9 x 12 pan with bread crumbs, then place a layer of eggplants over this. Cover with meat mixture, then add another layer of eggplants and meat again, until all is used, ending with eggplant.

Top with Cream Sauce No. 2 (page 3). Bake in oven 375-400° for 1 hour. Serves 6-7.

OKRA AND TOMATOES
"Bamyes me Tomatoes"

1 lb. okra	3 small onions chopped fine
1½ cups tomatoes, canned	1 tbsp. parsley chopped fine
½ cup olive oil	Salt and pepper
½ cup vinegar	

Wash okra and cut off stems, pour vinegar over them

in bowl and allow to stand for one hour. Rinse thoroughly in cold water, drain.

Brown onions in hot olive oil then add tomatoes and cook for three minutes. Add okra, parsley, salt, pepper and olive oil; and enough water to cover. Bring to a quick boil, then cook on low flame for 45 minutes. Serves 4.

MEAT RECIPES

To most Greek people, meat means lamb. It is the favorite meat for roast, stews, fricassée, and meat sauces.

At Easter time small whole lambs are either stuffed and roasted or cooked over open fires out of doors. In many homes, no other meat except lamb is used.

Next choice is veal, with beef third and pork rating very low in the Greek menus.

One of the characteristics of cooking meat Greek style is the use of tomatoes and tomato paste in most of the recipes. Onions are used for flavor and occasionally a bit of garlic to add to the tangy seasoning.

Chicken is one of the favorites of the Greek people, who have many varied recipes for the use of chicken.

Conspiciously absent in the preparation of meats, is the use of frying meats as is customary in America. All meats are lightly browned first and then cooked or baked in sauces.

LEG OF LAMB GRECIAN STYLE
"Arni Psito"

Leg of lamb 5-6 lbs.	4 cloves of garlic
1 large lemon	¼ cup butter
1 cup water	Salt and pepper

Wash meat and place in roasting pan. Mix salt and pepper and cloves of garlic. Make incisions in the lamb in several places and insert cloves of garlic, salt and pepper. Rub the salt, pepper and lemon over entire roast.

Cover and cook for one hour in oven 350°. Add one cup of water to the gravy, and baste roast during cooking, until meat is well browned.

Potatoes may be added to the gravy during the last thirty minutes of baking. Serves 7-8.

LAMB AND SPAGHETTI
"Arni me Spaghetti"

2½ lbs. lamb	1 No. 2 can tomatoes
1 lb. thin spaghetti	2 tbsp. tomato paste
1 large onion chopped fine	5 cups hot water
Salt and pepper	

Cut meat into serving pieces, wash thoroughly and place in baking pan. Add tomato, tomato paste, onions and 3 cups water and salt and pepper.

Cover and bake in 400° oven for 2 hours. Add remaining water and bring to a boil. Break spaghetti into small pieces and add to meat. Stir well, then cover and continue baking for 30 minutes, stirring occasionally while cooking.

Serve hot, sprinkle generously with grated cheese (kefaloteri). Serves 4-5.

LAMB WITH CELERY AND AVGOLEMONO SAUCE
"Arni me Selino Avgolemono"

2 lbs. stewing lamb
1 No. 2 can tomatoes
½ cup butter
1 large onion chopped
1½ cups water, hot
1 stalk celery
Salt and pepper

For Sauce: 2 eggs, ½ cup lemon juice and 3 tbsp. water.

Have meat cut into serving pieces. Wash well and saute in large pan for 5 minutes. Add butter and onions and brown for 10 minutes. Add tomatoes and cook over high flame for 5 minutes. Add hot water, salt and pepper to taste.

Reduce heat and cook for 1½ hours or until meat is tender. Cut celery into ½-inch pieces and add to meat.

Cover and continue cooking for 1 hour, or until celery is tender. Remove from flame. Prepare avgolemono sauce, using broth from meat. Pour over meat and stir carefully. Allow to stand 10 minutes. Serve hot. Serves 6-7.

LAMB WITH SMALL GREEN SQUASH
"Arni me Kolokethya"

2½ lbs. lamb
¼ cup butter
1 onion chopped fine
1 tbsp. chopped mint leaf
1 cup tomatoes (canned)
2 lbs. green squash sliced
1 garlic clove chopped
1 tbsp. chopped parsley
Salt and pepper

Wash and cut lamb into serving pieces and brown with onions in butter. Add tomatoes and one cup water, garlic, mint, parsley, salt and pepper. Cover and cook over low heat for 30 minutes.

Fry squash in olive oil until brown on all sides. Add to meat and continue cooking for 20 minutes, until meat is tender. Serves 5-6.

BAKED LAMB WITH MANESTRA

"Youvetsi"

2 lbs. lamb (chops or shoulder)	1 No. 2 can tomatoes
1 large onion chopped	1 tbsp. tomato paste
½ cup grated cheese (kaseri or kefaloteri)	2 cups manestra
8 cups hot water	Salt and pepper

Cut meat into serving pieces, wash thoroughly and place in roasting pan. Add onions, tomatoes, tomato paste, 3 cups water, and salt and pepper. Mix well, cover and bake in 400° oven for 1½ hours or until meat is tender.

Turn meat occasionally to brown on all sides. Add manestra and remaining 5 cups water. Mix well, cover, and continue baking for 35 minutes, stirring occasionally. Serve very hot. Sprinkle with grated cheese. Serves 5-6.

LAMB FRICASSÉE GREEK STYLE

"Arni Fricasse"

2½ lbs. very young lamb	3 stalks celery, leaves included (chopped)
2 large scallions (chopped)	3 carrots (chopped)
5 tbsp. anitho chopped fine	Salt and pepper
3 cups water	

Cut lamb into serving pieces and wash well. Place in large saucepan and add scallions, celery, carrots and water and boil over high flame for 15 minutes.

Remove scum from top of broth which forms during boiling process.

Remove vegetables and mash well together with a fork. Add to meat and also add anitho and season to taste. Bring to a boil, then reduce heat and cook for 50 minutes over low heat until meat is tender.

Prepare avgolemono sauce (page 2) and pour over

LAMB WITH RICE

"Arni Pilaffe"

2 lbs. lean lamb	1 tbsp. olive oil
1 large onion chopped fine	⅓ cup butter (½ stick)
1½ cups rice, long grain	3 tbsp. tomato paste
1 tsp. cinnamon	4½ cups water, hot

Salt and pepper

Wash and cut lamb into serving pieces. Brown well in large skillet, add onions and fry until onions are soft. Transfer to large saucepan. Blend tomato paste in one cup of water and add to meat, along with remaining water, olive oil, cinnamon, salt and pepper to taste. Cover and bring to boil over high flame. Reduce heat and cook for 1½ hours until tender.

Wash rice in cold water several times. Place in bowl with salt and hot water. Soak for 30 minutes. Drain well and roll in dish towel. Let stand 20 minutes. Place in skillet, add butter and fry for 10 minutes stirring constantly. Remove gravy from meat and measure, two parts liquid and one part rice. Add water to make enough liquid if needed.

Place back on high flame, bring to boil and add rice. Stir and cover. Reduce heat immediately and cook for 10 minutes on low. Do not remove cover at any time during cooking after rice has been added. Grasp saucepan in both hands and twist from side to side several times during cooking.

Remove from stove and allow to stand 10 minutes before serving. Serves 6.

[continued from previous recipe:] meat. Stir and allow to stand 10 minutes. Serve hot. Serves 4-5.

ROAST LAMB WITH POTATOES

"Psito Arni me Patates"

2 lbs. lamb
1 No. 2 can tomatoes
2½ cups water

7 medium potatoes cut quarters
Salt and pepper

Have meat cut into serving pieces. Arrange in roasting pan. Crush tomatoes and pour over meat, add water. Salt and pepper to taste. Bake in oven 500° for 1½ hours or until meat is tender. Turn meat occasionally. Add potatoes and continue baking for 35 minutes or until potatoes are done. Serve very hot. Serves 4-5.

OKRA AND LAMB STEW

"Bamyes me Arni"

2 lbs. lamb cut in small pieces and washed
2 lbs. okra, very small preferred
1 can tomato soup
1 tbsp. lamb fat

1 tbsp. salt
2 cups water
1 cup vinegar
1 tsp. salt

Cut the tops of okra. Wash, cover with 1 teaspoon salt and vinegar and let stand, stirring occasionally for 30 minutes.

Melt the fat in large pot. Add the meat. Stir until slightly brown. Add tomato and water and salt. Cook half an hour on low heat, or until meat is tender.

Add the okra with vinegar around the meat, keeping meat in center of pot. Do not stir, but grasping pot with two hands, shake gently from side to side. Allow to cook for 1 to 1½ hours. Let stand ½ hour before serving. Handle okra carefully so as to not break pieces. Serves 4.

LAMB WITH CAULIFLOWER

"Arni me Kounoupithi"

2½ lbs. lamb shoulder
3 small cauliflowers about 3 lbs.
1 No. 2 can tomatoes
1 large onion sliced thin
1 cup boiling water
⅓ cup butter (½ stick)
Salt and pepper

Cut cauliflower quarterly in bowl and add cold water until ready to use. Cut meat in serving pieces, wash thoroughly. Saute in frying-pan for 5 minutes. Add butter and brown well on all sides, turning occasionally to avoid burning. Transfer meat to large saucepan. In same butter, fry onions for 3 minutes stirring often. Add tomatoes, cover and simmer for 10 minutes. Pour over meat. Salt and pepper to taste.

Bring to a boil over high flame. Add 1 cup water and continue cooking for 1 hour on medium flame or until meat is tender. Drain cauliflower and add to meat. Cover and continue cooking for 35 minutes, until cauliflower is tender. Stir carefully to avoid breaking cauliflower. Serves 6-7.

STRING BEANS WITH LAMB

"Fasolia Fresca me Arni"

2 lbs. lamb
½ stick butter
1 No. 2 can tomatoes
1 large onion chopped
2 lbs. string beans
Salt and pepper

Have meat cut into serving pieces. Saute for 5 minutes in large skillet. Add butter and brown well. Transfer meat to saucepan and in same skillet and in remaining butter, brown onions for 6 minutes. Add tomatoes and cook over medium flame for 15 minutes. Salt and pepper to taste. Pour over meat, cover and cook for 1 hour, or until meat is tender.

In the meantime clean and wash string beans. Break in half, add to meat and continue cooking for 35 minutes until done. Serves 5-6.

LAMB WITH SPINACH
"Arni me Spanakia"

2 lbs. lamb	½ stick butter
Spinach, about 2 lbs.	1 No. 2 can tomatoes
2 large onions chopped fine	1½ cups water

Saute meat for 10 minutes in large saucepan, browning on all sides. Add butter and onions and brown for 10 minutes. Add tomatoes, salt and pepper and cover. Bring to a boil for 7 minutes. Add water and reduce heat to medium and cook for 1 hour and 20 minutes or until meat is tender.

In the meantime wash spinach thoroughly and cut into 3-inch pieces. Add to meat, stir well, cover and continue cooking for 30 minutes until tender. Serves 4-6.

LAMB KABOBS
"Arni Souvlakia"

4-5 lbs. loin of lamb	Salt and pepper
1 cup lemon juice	3 tomatoes medium size
Origano	

Cut meat into 1-inch pieces, dip into lemon juice and push onto skewer, placing half a tomato at each end. Season with salt and pepper with a dash of origano.

Cook over charcoal or under hot flame, turning occasionally for about 45 minutes until brown on all sides but not cooked dry. May be served with rice pilafe or as hors d'œuvres. 20-25 pieces.

Meat Recipes

LAMB KABOBS No. 2
"Arni Souvlakia"

Take two pounds of lamb and cut into 10 or 12 squares trying to keep even in size.

Season with salt, pepper and lemon juice and cook over an open grill.

Serve with salad or as an appetizer with crisp crackers and beverages. Serves 6.

ROAST LAMB WITH RICE
"Psito Arni me Rize"

3 lbs. lamb
2 cups long grain rice
Salt and pepper
6 firm tomatoes
½ cup butter

Have meat cut into serving pieces and season with salt and pepper. Place in shallow pan, cover with dabs of butter and place a heavy dish over meat.

Slice tomatoes and arrange around edges of meat. Bake in oven 250° until tender. Remove dish, add rice and four cups of boiling water. Cover.

Continue baking until rice is done—about 30 minutes. During cooking process, do not stir rice or meat. Turn pan swiftly from side to side during cooking, to keep from sticking. Serves 7-8.

BRAISED LAMB
"Yiahnisto Arni"

2 lbs. lean lamb
½ lemon
¼ cup butter
3 onions chopped fine
1 bay-leaf
Salt and pepper

Cut lamb into small cubes and brown lightly in butter. Remove meat and place in medium saucepan, then brown onions in remaining butter and pour over meat. Add enough water to cover, then add bay-leaf, salt and pepper to taste and lemon juice. Cover and cook on low flame for 2 hours.

This may be served with pilafi or manestra browned in butter. Serves 5-6.

ARTICHOKES AND LAMB STEW

Halki Style

"Arni me Aginares"

2 lbs lean lamb	Juice of 2 lemons
1 stick butter	2 cups water
6 small artichokes	Salt and pepper
2 medium onions chopped fine	

Peel artichokes and cut off tops. Wash well and let stand in juice of lemon for 30 minutes.

Saute meat and onions in butter until brown. Add water, cover and allow to simmer for 50 minutes. Add artichokes, cover and cook one hour until tender. Stir carefully so as to not break artichokes.

Serves 4-5.

OKRA AND LAMB STEW HALKI STYLE

"Bamyes me Arni"

1 lb. lamb	1 medium onion chopped fine
1 lb. okra	¼ cup olive oil
2 tbsp. tomato paste	1 lemon
1½ cups water	Salt and pepper
Vinegar	

Wash okra well, cut off stems, sprinkle with salt and soak in water and one tablespoon of vinegar for 30 minutes.

Saute the meat and onions in olive oil for 10 minutes

until well browned. Wash the okra in cold water and place in large saucepan.

Add tomatoes and onions, meat, tomato paste thinned out with water and the juice of one lemon. Salt and pepper to taste. Cook on low heat for 45 minutes in covered pan. Avoid stirring, but twist pan several times from side to side during cooking process. Serves 4-5.

LAMB AND TOMATO SAUCE
"Lamb Kapama"

2½ lbs. lamb
Juice of one lemon
1 cup hot water
Salt and pepper
¼ cup butter
1 No. 2 can tomatoes
Cinnamon to taste

Cut lamb into serving pieces and season with salt and pepper. Sprinkle with cinnamon and pour lemon juice over meat. Allow to stand for a few minutes, then brown in butter. Transfer meat from pan and add tomatoes, bringing to a boil and allow to simmer for 5 minutes.

Add meat and lemon juice which has been drained previously from the meat. Cook slowly for two hours. Add hot water slowly as needed. May be served with macaroni, rice or potatoes. Serves 4-5.

STUFFED EASTER LAMB HALKI STYLE
"Ardni Yemesto"

1 young lamb, 10 to 12 lbs.
1 lb. lean hamburger
Haslets from lamb (liver, heart, lung)
1 cup butter
3 cups long grain rice
4 cups water
½ stick butter
2 large onions grated
3 large lemons
1 tsp. cinnamon
2 tbsp. chopped mint-leaf
Salt and pepper

Chop livers, heart and lung very fine, add hamburger

and saute over high flame for 12 minutes, in a large skillet. Add butter and brown for 5 minutes, then add onions, rice and cinnamon and continue cooking for 5 minutes more. Add mint-leaf, 4 cups water and season to taste. Cover and cook for 10 minutes.

While filling is cooking, rub lamb inside well with ½ stick of butter and ½ of the lemon juice. Salt and pepper inside to taste.

When filling is done, begin stuffing lamb from the neck down, first sewing the lamb from the neck leaving a small opening at lower end to insert stuffing. When completely stuffed, rub remaining lemon juice and butter over outside of lamb. Salt and pepper well. Place in roasting pan, and add 2 cups water and bake at 400° for 2½ hours, basting occasionally with juice.

In many parts of Greece chestnuts and raisins are included in the stuffing, however this style shown above is most popular among the Greeks of the Dodecanese Islands.

BAKED MEAT AND POTATOES
"Kreas me Patates."

1 lb. hamburger	3 lbs. potatoes
2 large onions chopped fine	Salt and pepper
1 garlic clove	Butter

Boil potatoes, then peel and mash well, adding 1 tbsp. butter, salt and pepper.

Saute meat with onions for 5 minutes. Spread half the potatoes in a baking dish, cover with meat mixture, and top with remainder of potatoes. Dot with butter and bake in a moderate oven until well browned. Serves 4-5.

GREEK BEEF STEW

"Stifatho"

1½ lbs. lean beef	2 carrots sliced
8 small onions peeled	1 can tomato paste, 6 oz.
¼ cup butter	4½ cups boiling water
2 large potatoes cut in 3-inch cubes	1 tsp. cinnamon
	Salt and pepper

Cut meat into 1-inch cubes. Thin out tomato paste in two cups water. Saute meat for 5 minutes on high flame. Add butter and continue to brown for 3 minutes. Transfer to large saucepan.

In same skillet, brown onions lightly for 2 minutes.

Transfer to a bowl and keep covered until time to add meat.

In remaining butter add thinned tomato paste. Let come to boil over high flame. Add to meat along with 2½ cups water.

Cover and cook over medium flame for 1½ hours. Meat should now be done. Add carrots, potatoes, onions, cinnamon, salt and pepper to taste.

Cover and continue cooking for 35 minutes or until vegetables are done. Serve very hot. Serves 6-7.

BROILED STEAK GREEK STYLE

"Kreas me origano"

4 T-bone steaks	½ stick butter
2 lemons	Origano
Salt and pepper	

Wash meat thoroughly and place on broiler pan. Dot with butter, sprinkle with lemon juice, salt and pepper and origano.

When meat is done on one side, turn and proceed as

before. Cook until meat is brown and juicy, basting with pan juice. Before serving add more lemon juice and dot with remaining butter. Serve piping hot. Serves 4.

HAMBURG ROLLS
"Keftedes"

1¼ lb. hamburg	1 tsp. pepper
1 cup bread crumbs	5 eggs
3 tbsp. butter	Salt

Boil four of the eggs until hard. Mix meat, pepper, salt, one egg and half of the bread crumbs. Spread the meat mixture out in a large flat cake, keeping close together. Slice boiled eggs and arrange in the center of the meat. With floured hands roll meat up until a long roll is formed, with the eggs in the center.

Tie the roll in several places, so it will not come apart. Place in baking dish and bake in oven 350° until well browned. A small quantity of water may be added in the pan so the meat will not dry out.

Remove from oven and slice in thick slices. Serve hot. Serves 3-4.

MEAT-BALLS SMYRNA STYLE
"Keftedes Smyrneikes"

1½ lbs. hamburg	4 oz. cracker-meal
1 large onion chopped fine	½ cup olive oil
2 garlic cloves chopped fine	Salt and pepper
3 eggs well beaten	1 tsp. cinnamon
1 tsp. anise	

Mix all ingredients well and shape into small balls. Fry in hot olive oil until light brown. Place in saucepan, cover with sauce and cook in a covered pan for ½ hour over low heat. Serve with rice or spaghetti.

Meat Recipes

Sauce Recipe

1 6-oz. can tomato paste Salt and pepper
1½ cups water

Mix ingredients and pour over meat-balls. Serves 4-5.

BAKED MEAT-BALLS
"Keftethes sto Fournou."

2 medium onions chopped fine
1 lb. ground beef
2 tbsp. thiosmo (mint-leaf) chopped fine
¼ cup butter
1 cup toast crumbs
1½ cups water
1 No. 2 can tomatoes
½ tsp. cinnamon
Salt and pepper

In a large bowl, combine meat, onions, mint-leaf, toast crumbs, water, salt and pepper. Mix well and shape into egg-shaped balls. Arrange in small baking dish.

Strain tomatoes through sieve and pour over meat-balls. Top with pieces of butter, sprinkle with cinnamon.

Bake in oven 400° for 1 hour, turning balls occasionally so they may brown on all sides. Serve hot with rice pilafe or buttered spaghetti. Serves 4.

GREEK MEAT-BALLS
"Keftedes"

1 lb. hamburger
2 medium chopped onions
1 cup crushed light brown bread crumbs
1½ cups olive oil
1 cup flour
2 tbsp. mint-leaf chopped fine
1 lemon
2½ cups of water or
  1 No. 2 can tomatoes
Salt and pepper

Mix all ingredients except oil and flour. Add salt and pepper to taste and mix well.

Take one tablespoonful at a time and roll in flour, shaping into small balls.

Shake off excess flour and fry in very hot olive oil, over medium flame for 10 minutes or until brown on both sides.

Transfer to large bowl or platter and keep warm until served. Sprinkle with juice of lemon. Serve hot or cold. Serves 5-6.

"These 'Keftedes' are served at all festive gatherings, weddings, baptism parties, engagement parties and are a great picnic favorite. They may be kept for hours and still retain their fine flavor, unlike ordinary meat-balls."

SPAGHETTI WITH GROUND MEAT SAUCE
"Makaronia me Kima Saltsa."

1 lb. fine spaghetti
1 lb. ground beef
2 large onions chopped fine
1 stick butter
1½ cups hot water
3 garlic cloves sliced thin
2 bay-leaves
1 cup canned tomatoes
4 tbsp. tomato paste
1 tsp. cinnamon
3 tsps. olive oil
Salt and pepper

Saute meat for 5 minutes. Add onions, garlic, butter and oil. Brown well for 8 minutes stirring constantly. Add tomato paste, tomatoes, bay-leaves, salt and pepper to taste and bring to a boil.

Reduce heat and cook for 30 minutes. Cook spaghetti as shown on page 31.

Arrange spaghetti on large platter and sprinkle layers with grated Kefaloteri cheese. Spread meat sauce on top. Serve hot. Serves 6-7.

SPAGHETTI WITH HAMBURGER SAUCE
"Greek Spaghetti"

1 lb. spaghetti
1 large onion chopped fine
1 lb. hamburger
1 8-oz. can tomatoe paste
1 tsp. cinnamon
1 stick butter
2 garlic cloves chopped fine
Salt and pepper
Grated Kefaloteri cheese

Thin out tomato paste with water. Brown hamburger and onion in butter about 10 minutes. Add tomato paste, cinnamon, garlic, salt and pepper to taste. Add one cup of water and cook over low flame for ¾ hour until sauce is thick.

Cook buttered spaghetti (page 31). Arrange on large platter, alternating with meat sauce in one layer and spaghetti until all is used, ending with spaghetti then meat. Sprinkle generously with cheese. Serve hot. Serves 5-6.

MEAT-BALLS AND SPAGHETTI
"Youverlakia me Spaghetti"

1 lb. ground beef
2 medium size onions chopped fine
1 garlic clove chopped fine
Grated Kefaloteri cheese
⅔ cup toast crumbs
¼ cup water
2 cups olive oil
Salt and pepper

Sauce Ingredients:

1 can tomato paste, 6 oz.
1 cup canned tomatoes
1 tsp. cinnamon
¼ cup butter
2 cups hot water
1 garlic clove sliced thin

Put tomato paste in large saucepan. Strain tomatoes through sieve into paste. Add garlic, water, cinnamon, butter, salt and pepper to taste. Mix well. Cover and bring to boil over high flame. Reduce heat and cook 30 minutes.

While sauce is cooking, prepare meat-balls as follows: Mix meat, onions, garlic, toast crumbs, water, salt and pepper, until well blended and form into egg-shaped balls. Fry in very hot olive oil about 3 minutes until golden brown on all sides. Place in boiling sauce, cover and cook for 10 minutes. Prepare spaghetti as directed on page 31.

Arrange spaghetti and sauce in layers on large platter, sprinkling cheese in between each layer. Top with sauce and meat-balls. Serve very hot. Serves 5-6.

MEAT-BALLS WITH AVGOLEMONO SAUCE

"Uverlakia Avgolemono"

2 lbs. ground beef
2 large onions chopped fine
1 qt. water
1 No. 2 can tomatoes, strained

½ cup rice
½ cup butter
Salt and pepper

Sauce Ingredients:

4 eggs   4 tsp. water
Juice of 2 lemons

Wash rice thoroughly and place in large bowl. Add meat, onions, tomatoes, salt and pepper to taste. Mix well. In the meantime bring water, tomatoes and butter to a boil over high flame. Make small balls of the meat mixture and drop them into the water while it is boiling.

Reduce heat, cover and cook for 20 minutes. Remove from stove and pour off all gravy from meat-balls. Prepare Avgolemono Sauce (page 2). Pour sauce over meat-balls and serve hot. Serves 5-6.

Meat Recipes

MEAT-BALLS WITH AVGOLEMONO SAUCE

Youverlakia (Constantinople Style)

1 cup diced carrots	2 lemons
1 cup canned tomatoes	3 small potatoes
½ cup butter	2½ cups water
⅓ cup long grain rice	2 lb. hamburger
1 cup diced celery	1 onion chopped
3 eggs	Salt and pepper

Cook carrots, celery and butter in water for 30 minutes, then strain well through a strainer, placing pulp in a bowl to be used later.

Mix rice, tomatoes, hamburger, onion, salt and pepper and form into small balls the size of an egg. Drop into strained broth, and cut potatoes over them. Then add strained vegetables. Cover and cook over low flame for 20 minutes.

Prepare Avgolemono Sauce (page 2) with 3 eggs, and juice of 2 lemons.

Pour over meat and allow to stand 10 minutes before serving. Serves 6.

MEAT LOAF AND POTATOES

"Mousakas me Patates"

2 lbs. lean ground beef	2 eggs well beaten
½ cup butter	2 cups boiling water
1 can tomato paste, 6-oz.	½ cup grated cheese
1 tsp. cinnamon	½ cup olive oil ⎱ for frying
6 potatoes sliced	½ cup butter ⎰
2 onions (chopped)	Salt and pepper

Thin out tomato paste with 1 cup water. Saute hamburger for 10 minutes. Add butter and onions and fry for 10 minutes stirring occasionally. Add tomato paste, cinnamon, 1 cup water, salt and pepper. Cover and cook 15 minutes over medium flame.

Brown potatoes in butter and oil until light brown for 3 minutes. Arrange in bottom of pan half of potatoes, making sure that they are placed close together. Spread meat over this. Arrange remaining potatoes over meat and top with cream sauce No. 1 (page 3).

Sprinkle top with 2 tablespoons grated Kefaloteri cheese and cinnamon to taste. Bake in 450° oven for 25 minutes. Cool before cutting. Cut into ⅔-inch square pieces. Remove carefully with spatula to avoid breaking. Serve warm. Serves 16.

MANESTRA WITH GROUND BEEF

"Manestra me Kima"

1 lb. ground beef	3 tbsp. tomato paste
1 large onion chopped fine	1 tbsp. olive oil
1½ cups tomatoes, canned	1 tsp. cinnamon
2 cups manestra	5 cups hot water
½ cup butter	Salt and pepper

Brown meat in large pot for 5 minutes. Add onions and butter and continue browning for 5 more minutes, stirring occasionally. Add tomato paste, tomatoes, oil, cinnamon, 3 cups water, salt and pepper. Cover and cook over medium flame for 20 minutes.

Add manestra and remaining 2 cups water. Bring to a boil, reduce to low flame, and cook covered for 20 minutes, until manestra is tender. Serve very hot, sprinkle with grated cheese before serving. Serves 6-7.

BRAISED LIVER (HASLETS)

"Sikoti Yaihni"

2 lbs. haslets (liver, spleen and heart)
2 large onions chopped fine
½ cup butter
1 No. 2 can tomatoes
1½ cups hot water
Salt and pepper

Cut meat into 1-inch pieces. Wash thoroughly. In a large pan, saute for 10 minutes with butter, stirring occasionally to avoid burning.

Add onions, butter and cover. Cook for 12 minutes until brown. Add tomato and water, salt and pepper to taste. Stir well, cover and bring to a boil for three minutes. Cook over medium heat for 1 hour or until tender. Serve very hot, with rice or manestra and butter. Serves 4-5.

SAVORY SIDE DISH

"Sfogato"

1 lb. lamb hamburger
1 lb. small green squash cubed
Pinch of pepper
2 tsp. parsley chopped fine
8 eggs
3 onions chopped fine
4 tbsp. butter
½ tsp. salt
2 cups water

Combine all in frying-pan and cook until thick and meat is done. Beat eggs until fluffy and fold into hamburg mixture.

Pour into baking dish and bake in moderate oven 375° until firm. Serves 4-5.

BEEF STEW WITH ONIONS
"Stifatho"

2 lbs. lean beef	1 tbsp. wine or vinegar (optional)
1 No. 2 can tomatoes	18 small onions
½ cup butter	3 cups hot water
1 tsp. pickle spices (omit peppers)	Salt and pepper

Have meat cut into 2-inch squares. Wash well. Peel onions, being careful not to cut off lower part, so onions will remain whole.

Saute meat in large skillet for 15 minutes. Add butter and brown for 5 minutes on all sides. Transfer to large saucepan. In same skillet, brown onions lightly. Transfer to bowl and cover to use later with meat. Again in same skillet, add tomatoes to cook 5 minutes. Pour over meat. Add spices, wine if preferred. Salt and pepper to taste. Add water, stir, then cover and bring to boil over high flame. Reduce heat and cook for 1½ hours or until meat is tender. Add onions and continue cooking for one hour. Serve hot. Serves 5-6.

ROAST PORK LOIN WITH POTATOES
"Psito Hirino me Patates"

4 lbs. pork loin	2 lemons
4 garlic cloves	7 large potatoes
9 cups hot water	Salt and pepper

Wash pork loin. With point of sharp knife, make small slits in side and insert cloves of garlic. Rub lightly with juice of lemon. Salt and pepper to taste.

Place in roasting pan, add half of water and bake in oven 500° for 1 hour. Reduce heat to 375°, add remaining water and continue cooking for 45 minutes until tender and golden brown on all sides.

Remove loin and keep warm. Add potatoes to pan juice and salt and pepper well. Bake for 35 minutes until tender and brown. Serve very hot. Serves 7-8.

PIG FEET HALKI STYLE
"Pihti" (Hirina Potharakia)

4 pig's feet, medium size, tender	1 cup lemon juice
3 quarts water	1 heaping tbsp. flour
1 garlic clove	Salt and pepper

Have pig's feet thoroughly clean and place in water with garlic and cook over medium flame for 3½ hours. Remove from flame.

Dissolve flour in lemon juice, add salt and pepper and pour sufficient hot water from saucepan into lemon juice to form a thin paste, then pour this into pig's feet and remaining broth.

Pour contents of saucepan into large bowl. Salt and pepper to taste. Cool and place in refrigerator for 1 or 2 hours until it begins to congeal. Serve cold. Serves 4.

VEAL HALKI STYLE
"Stefatho"

2 lbs. stewing veal	½ cup vinegar
14-15 small onions	2 cups water
2 cloves of garlic	1 No. 2 can tomatoes
½ cup butter	1 bay-leaf
Salt and pepper	

Melt butter in frying-pan and brown meat cubes thoroughly. Place in medium saucepan. Brown garlic and onions in remaining butter and season with spices.

Dilute vinegar and water and tomatoes and pour over meat mixture together with onions and garlic. Cover and cook over low heat for two hours.

Do not remove cover during cooking process, but twist saucepan from side to side several times to keep from scorching. Serves 4-5.

RABBIT STEW
"Stifatho Lagos"

1 med. size rabbit (5-6 lbs.)	2 cups water
12 small onions	½ cup pure olive oil
1 can thick tomato soup	½ head garlic chopped fine
1 tsp. ground cloves	1 cup seedless raisins
1 tsp. nutmeg	3 bay-leaves

Salt and pepper

Wash rabbit thoroughly and cut into serving pieces. Arrange in baking dish, add all ingredients, cover tightly and bake in 325° oven for 4 hours or until tender, stirring occasionally, being careful not to break the rabbit or onions. Serve hot. Serves 5-6.

Note: If wild rabbit is used, soak overnight in vinegar before using. Beef tongue may be substituted for the rabbit if desired. Be sure the skin is removed carefully from tongue before cooking.

FOWL RECIPES

CHICKEN WITH RICE

"Kota me Rize."

1 broiler, 3 lbs.	1 tsp. cinnamon
2 onions chopped fine	1½ cups canned tomatoes
⅓ cup olive oil	3 cups boiling water
1 cup rice	Salt and pepper

Wash chicken thoroughly and cut into serving pieces. Brown in saucepan with olive oil, then add onion, cinnamon, tomato and season to taste. Cover and cook one hour over low flame, with one cup water.

Add rice and 3 cups water and cook over low flame until rice is tender. More water may be added if needed. Stir occasionally very carefully so as to not break up chicken pieces. Let stand 10 minutes before serving. Serves 4.

CHICKEN WITH OKRA

"Kotopoulo me Bamyes"

1 broiler, 5-6 lbs.	2 tbsp. tomato paste
1½ cups water	½ stick butter
1½ lbs. okra	Salt and pepper

Place chicken in a roasting pan and bake at 375° until done. Remove from oven and break into pieces. Place in casserole with butter, tomato paste and seasoning. Arrange the okra around chicken. Simmer over medium flame for 1 hour until done. Serve hot. Seaves 5.

BAKED CHICKEN GREEK STYLE

"Chicken Riganata"

1 chicken, about 5 lbs.	¼ tsp. origano
2 tbsp. melted butter	Juice of ½ lemon
2 cups water	Salt and pepper
2 tbsp. olive oil	

Clean chicken thoroughly, rub with lemon juice, salt and pepper to taste. Add remaining ingredients. Cover. Bake 375° 1½ hours, baste while cooking. Serves 4-5.

STEWED CHICKEN

"Kota Kapama"

1 spring chicken 5-6 lbs.	¼ lb. butter
¼ tsp. cloves	3 tbsp. olive oil
1½ cups canned tomatoes	Juice of one lemon
2 tbsp. tomato paste	Salt and pepper
1 tsp. cinnamon	2 cups water

Wash chicken and cut into serving pieces. Mix lemon juice, cloves, cinnamon and salt and pepper and rub into each piece of chicken. Brown chicken lightly in hot butter and oil. Remove from pan. Then add tomatoes, tomato paste and water. Cook for 15 minutes over low flame. Pour sauce over chicken.

Cook for approximately 1½ hours until chicken is well done.

May be served with spaghetti or rice. Serves 6-8.

BUTTERED CHICKEN WITH POTATOES
"Psito Kotopoulo"

1 fryer or broiler, about 4 lbs.	9 med. potatoes quartered
1½ cups water	Juice of 1 lemon
½ cup butter	Origano
Salt and pepper	

Wash fryer well, and cut into serving pieces. Arrange in small baking dish and arrange potatoes around fryer. Sprinkle generously with origano. Put dabs of butter on fryer and potatoes. Add water, salt and pepper to taste and top with lemon juice. Bake in medium oven for 50 minutes, until golden brown and tender. Baste occasionally with juice in pan. Serve hot. Serves 5-6.

CHICKEN WITH SPAGHETTI
"Kota me Spaghetti"

1 fryer, 2-3 lbs.	2 garlic cloves chopped
1 medium onion chopped fine	3⅓ cups water
1 6-oz. can tomato paste	1 tsp. cinnamon
½ stick butter (¼ cup)	½ tsp. mixed spices
Salt and pepper	(omit peppers)

Cut chicken into serving pieces and wash thoroughly. Thin out tomato paste with two cups water. Brown chicken slightly in butter for about 10 minutes. Transfer to saucepan. In skillet add remaining butter and saute onion three minutes. Add tomato paste; simmer 2 minutes. Pour over chicken. Add cinnamon, garlic and 1 cup water. Salt and pepper to taste.

Reduce heat to medium and cover. Cook for 45 minutes, or until chicken is tender. Stir occasionally being careful not to break chicken. Serve chicken on large platter.

Cook spaghetti and butter as shown on page 31. Top with sauce from chicken. Serves 5-6.

CHICKEN WITH PEAS
"Kota me Bizelia"

1 fryer, about 3 lbs.	1 cup water
1 No. 2 can tomatoes	½ cup butter
2½ lbs. fresh green peas	1 large onion chopped fine

Cut fryer into serving pieces and saute in large saucepan for 5 minutes. Add butter and onions and fry for about 6 minutes. Add tomato, salt and pepper to taste, cover and cook for 10 minutes. Add water and continue cooking for 1 hour or until chicken is tender.

In the meantime shell and wash peas, and add to chicken stirring carefully to avoid breaking the chicken pieces. Cover and continue cooking 30 minutes until peas are tender. Serve hot. Serves 4-5.

TURKEY DODECANESE STYLE
"Turkos Gemistos"

12-lb. turkey	Turkey livers chopped fine
1 lb. hamburger	2½ cups rice, long grain
½ lb. butter	2 tbsp. tomato paste
3 cups water	1 tbsp. cinnamon
4 tbsp. chopped mint-leaf	3 large lemons
5 med. onions (chopped)	Salt and pepper

Have turkey cleaned and washed thoroughly. Rub well

inside and out with lemon juice, salt and pepper to taste and allow to stand for 20-25 minutes while preparing the following stuffing.

Saute livers and hamburger for 10 minutes. Add butter and fry until brown. Add onions and continue frying for 5 minutes. Add rice, cinnamon, tomato paste, thinned out with water (1 cup); mint-leaf, salt and pepper to taste.

Cook over medium flame for 10 minutes stirring occasionally. Allow to cool, then stuff turkey well, and sew up.

Place in roasting pan and add 2 cups water. Bake in oven 500° for one hour. Reduce heat to 375° and cook two hours.

During the last 30 minutes of cooking potatoes may be placed around the turkey in gravy. Serves 8-10.

Greek Easter Food Customs

THE celebration of Easter by the Greek people throughout the world, brings to mind the many unusual customs observed in the Greek homes regarding various foods and their preparations.

Beginning with Palm Sunday, only fish is served in the home on that day, which marks the start of Holy Week fasting. It is during this week, that all foods are eliminated which are from anything living. This includes besides meats; eggs, milk, cheese, butter and fish. A great many of the more devout, older people eliminate olive oil also.

Unlike the Anglo-Saxon method of dying eggs many different colors, the Greeks dye their eggs only a deep blood red; which signifies the blood of Christ. They are dyed as a good luck token in the home, and are dyed only on Holy Thursday and Saturday. Any other day of the week, particularly Good Friday, is considered bad luck.

However, by the same token, Good Friday is chosen as the only day that Easter loaves of bread may be baked. These thick, round loaves, decorated with bright red eggs stuck in the dough are also considered good luck in the home. The observance of baking on Good Friday is observed in the homes as well as in commercial Greek bread bakeries. Tiny loaves containing one egg are made for the children of the family and friends.

Crisp doughnut-shaped cookies known as "Koulourakia" are one of the favorites of the Greeks and are served to callers during Holy Week. The dry, crisp cakes, covered with powdered sugar and known as "Kourambiethes" are also served at Easter time; particularly if there is a male member of the family whose namesake day comes on Easter. This would apply to those names derived from "Anastasis" meaning the "Resurrection."

With the observance of the Resurrection services at midnight at the Greek Orthodox churches, the family returns home to partake of an especially prepared soup known as "Mageritsa", which is made from the liver, heart and lungs of the lamb; well-cooked and seasoned with a lemon sauce. Fasts are broken with the eating of this soup, and on Easter the preparations for the roasting of the traditional lamb are under way.

Small, whole lambs are generally used, and some are roasted out-of-doors on open spits as they were in Greece. Others are baked at home, while in localities where Greek bakeries are found, they are baked along with the loaves of Greek bread. Stuffing the lamb, not unlike the stuffing of a turkey, is one tasty method of serving Easter lamb.

The head of the lamb is usually cooked separately in the oven until crisp and brown, and is considered a delicacy.

When the family gathers at the table for the Easter meal, the ancient custom of egg-cracking begins. The head of the family selects an egg from the bowl and turning to the person seated on his right, tries to crack the egg held tightly in the hand so that only the tip shows. If he successfully cracks that one, he continues on down the table, until his egg cracks. That is the sign for the rest of the family to join in the egg cracking.

Once again Easter is over, and normal eating begins for the family until the following year.

FISH AND OTHER SEAFOOD RECIPES

On the following pages a cross section of fish recipes are given, ranging from fried fish, Greek style, to stuffed squids, the latter prepared in an intricate fashion.

The Greek people, following the Orthodox faith, serve fish on Friday in their homes, observing the custom faithfully.

FRIED FISH MARINATA

3 lbs. fish (any kind)
Olive oil for frying
1¼ cups water
½ cup vinegar or wine
4 garlic buds
1 cup flour
Salt and pepper
2 tbsp. tomato paste
2 bay-leaves
1 tsp. black laurel rosemary

Clean and wash fish well. Cut into serving pieces, salt

and pepper to taste. Let stand 15 minutes then roll in flour and fry in deep fat over medium flame until golden brown on both sides. When done place in deep dish.

Brown flour lightly in skillet then add remainder of ingredients and cook for 15 minutes over low flame. Pour over fish and serve. Serves 6-7.

FISH ROE SALAD

"Tarama Salada"

One 7-oz. jar Tarama	2 cups toast crumbs rolled fine
1 cup olive oil	Parsley and Greek olives for garnish
1 onion chopped fine	
Juice of 2 lemons	

Place tarama in lukewarm water and allow to stand for 10 minutes. Remove membranes and scales.

With rotary beater mix tarama until it becomes a smooth paste, then add bread crumbs and onion, continuing to beat until it becomes light and well blended.

Add olive oil and lemon juice stirring constantly until a smooth paste is formed. If saltier salad preferred, use 1 cup crumbs.

Serve in a bowl garnished with olives and parsley, or may be used on hors d'œuvres.

CRABS AND RICE

"Kavouria Pilaffe"

6 large crabs	1½ cups long grain rice
1 large onion chopped fine	1 No. 2 can tomatoes
½ cup olive oil	Salt and pepper

Tear large claws from crab and break in two. Discard small claws. With point of knife remove body from back shell. Wash thoroughly to remove foreign particles. If roe is present in shell, remove and use also, as it enhances the flavor. Break body in two.

Saute onion in olive oil for 5 minutes. Strain tomato through fine sieve and add to onions, cook for 5 minutes, salt and pepper to taste. Add claws, bodies of crabs and roe. Cook 5 minutes.

Measure liquid. It should be two parts water and one part rice. If more water is needed to liquid to make two parts, it may be added to gravy.

Cook on high flame, add water and bring to boil. Add rice which has been thoroughly washed. Stir well, reduce heat to low, and continue cooking for 10 minutes, in covered pan. Do not remove cover during cooking, but turn pot several times from side to side to prevent scorching. Remove from fire and allow to stand 10 minutes before serving.

STEWED SNAILS
"Karavoli Yiahni"

2 lbs. snails	1 tbsp. tomato paste
3 large onions (chopped	½ cup olive oil
1 No. 2 can tomatoes	¾ cup hot water
1 tbsp. salt	Salt and pepper

Place snails in large deep saucepan. Cover with cold water and let stand overnight. Be sure cover is on tightly. Wash snails several times, place in 2 quarts salted water. Bring to a boil and remove immediately, drain. Pour oil in deep saucepan. Add onion and cook 12 minutes or until soft. Add tomato paste and tomato, salt and pepper to taste.

Cover and cook over medium flame for ten minutes. Add snails and ¾ cup water. Stir and cook 20 minutes. Serve very hot with sauce. (Use small oyster fork or nut pick to extract snails.) Serves 4-5.

BROILED TROUT WITH LEMON SAUCE
"Psito Psari"

4 small whole trout, about 3 lbs.	Origano to taste
2 lemons	Salt and pepper

Wash fish well and sprinkle fish inside and out with lemon juice, salt and pepper and let stand 30 minutes.

Drain and broil at low oven for 40 minutes turning occasionally with spatula to avoid breaking.

When done place in pyrex baking dish and top with sauce as follows:

Take ¾ cup lemon juice and ½ cup pure olive oil and beat with rotary beater for 25 minutes until light and fluffy. Pour over fish and let stand 10 minutes before serving. Sprinkle with origano. Serve hot. Serves 6-7.

BROILED TROUT GREEK STYLE
"Psari me Origano"

2 large trout	Salt and pepper
2 lemons	Origano
½ stick butter	

Have fish cut into filets and place on broiler pan. Salt and pepper well on meaty side. Dot with butter and squeeze juice of one lemon over filets. Sprinkle with origano.

Broil under flame 400° until fish begins to brown lightly. Baste with juice, add more butter and lemon juice as needed. When done remove to hot platter. Dot with remaining butter, sprinkle with origano and serve hot. Lemon slices may be used to garnish fish.

This fish is delicious served with the Greek salad given on page 16. Serves 4.

FISH ROE CAKES
"Tarama Keftedes"

1 7-oz. can tarama	Flour
5 medium potatoes boiled and peeled	1 tbsp. mint chopped fine
	1 tbsp. parsley chopped fine
Olive oil to fry	Salt and pepper
1 onion grated	

Place tarama in warm water for 10 minutes then rinse and remove membranes and scales. Place in large bowl and mix with rotary beater to thin paste. Mash potatoes thoroughly and add to tarama, blending well. Add onion and remainder of ingredients and mix well.

Form into patties and roll in flour. Fry in hot olive oil until well browned. Serves 4.

SCALLOPS WITH RICE
"Htenia Pilaffe"

1 qt. medium size scallops	1½ cups rice, long grain
¾ cup olive oil	3 cups boiling water
1 large onion sliced fine	Salt and pepper
⅓ cup butter (½ stick)	

Wash scallops thoroughly. Brown onion in olive oil until golden brown and add scallops. Cover and cook over medium flame for 25 minutes, stirring occasionally.

Prepare rice as follows: Wash rice in cold water several times. Place in bowl with salt and hot water. Soak for 30 minutes. Drain well. Roll in dish towel and let stand 20 minutes. Place in skillet, add butter and fry for 10 minutes, stirring constantly. Remove gravy from scallops and measure, two parts liquid and one part rice. Add water to gravy if needed to make two parts.

Place back on flame, bring to boil and add rice. Stir

and cover, and immediately reduce heat to cook 10 minutes on low. Do not remove cover at any time after rice has been added. To avoid scorching, grasp saucepan with both hands and twist several times from side to side occasionally.

Remove from stove. Stir and let stand 10 minutes before serving. Serves 5-6.

BAKED FISH
"Psito Psari"

1 whole grouper, abt. 3 lbs.	3 large onions chopped fine
¾ cup olive oil	2 garlic cloves chopped fine
Juice of 2 lemons	½ cup water
1 lemon sliced	Salt and pepper

½ tsp. chopped parsley ⎫ for stuffing
½ tsp. origano ⎭

Clean fish and slit down center. Sprinkle inside with lemon juice. Salt and pepper and let stand 20 minutes. Drain and place in baking dish and stuff with parsley and origano. Saute onions and garlic lightly 3 minutes in olive oil. Pour over fish. Arrange sliced lemon on top of fish, add water and bake in oven 375° for 45-50 minutes or until fish is tender. Baste occasionally with pan juice. Serves 4-5.

FISH PATTIES
"Psari Keftedes"

2 cups cooked fish meat	1 cup toast crumbs
1 tbsp. mint-leaf chopped fine	1 cup flour
2 lemons	¾ cup water
1 large onion chopped fine	⅓ cup grated cheese
2 eggs	Olive oil for frying.

Salt and pepper

Mash fish very fine with fork. Add mint-leaf, onion,

Fish and Other Seafood Recipes 81

eggs, toast crumbs, grated cheese and water. Salt and pepper to taste and mix thoroughly. Form into small patties about 2 inches in diameter.

Roll in flour and fry in very hot olive oil about 5 minutes or until golden brown on both sides. Serve very hot. Sprinkle with lemon juice. Serves 5-6.

SHRIMP AND RICE
"Garides Pilafi"

2 lbs. shrimp shelled and washed
1 stick butter
2 medium onions chopped fine
½ cup olive oil
1 No. 2 can tomatoes
1½ cups long grain rice
Salt and pepper

Saute onion in olive oil over medium flame for 10 minutes. Add tomato and stir. Cover and cook about 3 minutes. Add shrimp, salt and pepper to taste, stir well and cover. Cook for 6 minutes. Remove from stove and pour off gravy from shrimp, so as to have two parts liquid and one part rice, add water if necessary.

Wash rice in cold water several times. Place in bowl with salt and hot water. Soak for 30 minutes. Drain well and roll in dish towel. Let stand 20 minutes. Put rice into skillet, add butter and cook for 10 minutes stirring constantly. Add to shrimps. Bring to boil on high, stir and cover. Reduce heat immediately and cook for 10 minutes on low. Do not remove cover at any time during cooking after rice has been added. Grasp saucepan in both hands and twist from side to side several times during cooking.

Remove from stove and allow to stand 10 minutes before serving. Serves 6-7.

BRAISED SHRIMP

"Garides Yiahni"

2 lbs. shrimp unshelled	3 tbsp. parsley or anitho chopped
3 medium onions (chopped)	2 tbsp. tomato paste
1 cup tomatoes crushed	
Salt and pepper	

Wash shrimp well, drain. Saute onions in large saucepan with olive oil for 5 minutes. Add tomato paste and tomatoes, cook over medium flame for 3 minutes. Add parsley or anitho and continue cooking for 3 minutes. Add shrimp, salt and pepper to taste.

Cover and cook for 15 minutes or until shrimp are tender and can be removed easily from shell. Serve very hot. Serves 5-6.

FRIED SHRIMP GREEK STYLE

"Garides Teganestes"

1 lb. shrimp with heads and tails removed	Juice of 1 lemon
½ stick butter	Salt and pepper
½ cup olive oil	1 cup flour

Clean shrimp thoroughly, split backs and remove spine. Roll shrimp in flour and fry in hot olive oil and butter, until light brown.

Serve hot with juice of lemon sprinkled on them. May be served with a shrimp sauce if desired. Serves 4.

BAKED FISH AND VEGETABLES

"Plaki Psari"

2 whole trout with heads (4 lbs.)
¾ cup olive oil
2 large onions sliced lengthwise
1 lemon
1 large carrot sliced
1 No. 2 can tomatoes
3 celery stalks (leaves included) chopped
2 tbsp. chopped parsley
1 small green pepper chopped
Salt and pepper

Clean fish thoroughly. Sprinkle with lemon juice and salt and let stand 30 minutes. Arrange in baking pan. Fry onion in large skillet for 5 minutes. Add parsley, celery, carrots, pepper and cook over high flame for 5 minutes. Add tomatoes, salt and pepper to taste.

Cover and cook over medium flame for 20 minutes. Add ¼ cup water and continue cooking 10 minutes. Stir occasionally. Pour over fish and bake in 400° oven for 35 minutes. Serve very hot. Serves 6.

FRIED DRY COD AND GARLIC DRESSING

"Bakalieros Teganetos"

1 whole dry cod (3-lb.)
1 cup flour
Pepper to taste
1 cup olive oil

Cut fish into 4-inch pieces; soak overnight. Change water several times. Wash again in cold water before cooking.

Dry, roll in flour and fry 4 or 5 minutes in hot olive oil or until light brown on each side.

Serve either hot or cold with 1 teaspoon of garlic dressing or serve hot with green vegetables. Serves 4-5.

SQUIDS WITH RICE

"Kalamaria me Rize"

2 lbs. small squids	¾ cup olive oil
1 large onion chopped fine	1 No. 2 can tomatoes, strained
2 cups long grain rice	½ stick butter

Remove ink sac and bones from squid. Wash thoroughly. Remove head and entrails from body. Cut into tiny pieces and saute in large saucepan for 10 minutes. Pour off broth from squids and save for use later. Continue to saute for 10 minutes more.

Add chopped onion and cook for 5 minutes. Add strained tomatoes and broth from squids. Salt and pepper to taste. Bring to a boil and cover. Cook over medium flame for half hour. Add ½ cup water and continue cooking for 1 hour or until squids are tender.

In the meantime prepare rice with butter as for pilaffe.

Pour off two parts gravy from squid and one part rice, adding water if needed. Cook over low flame for 10 minutes. Serve hot. Serves 6.

STUFFED SQUIDS

"Kalamaria Gemista"

5 lbs. medium size squids	¾ cup olive oil
2 medium onions chopped fine	2 tbsp. tomato paste
2 tbsp. chopped thiosmo (mint-leaf)	1 cup canned tomatoes
	¼ cup water
½ cup long grain rice	Salt and pepper

Remove ink sac and bones from squid. Wash thoroughly. Remove head and remove entrails from body. Cut feelers from head and place them with entrails on board. Chop fine and place in bowl. Add rice, ½ cup olive oil, mint-leaf, tomato paste, tomatoes, salt and pepper to taste and mix well. Stuff squids and replace heads to keep filling from coming out.

Arrange in baking dish and pour remaining juice from stuffing over squids. Add remaining oil and water and bake in hot oven 475° for 20 minutes. Reduce heat to 375° and continue for 30 minutes or until rice is tender. Base occasionally with broth. Serve very hot. Serves 7-8.

BRAISED FISH
"Psari Yiahni"

1 whole trout (2-3 lbs.), other fish may be substituted
½ cup olive oil
4 very ripe tomatoes chopped
2 large onions sliced thin lengthwise
4 tbsp. chopped parsley
Juice of one lemon
Salt and pepper

Have fish cleaned and washed well. Sprinkle inside and out with lemon juice, salt and pepper and let stand for 30 minutes. Cut into 2-inch pieces. Saute onions in large saucepan with olive oil for 5 minutes.

Add tomatoes and parsley and cook over medium flame for 30 minutes until sauce is thick. Add fish and continue cooking 20 minutes. Avoid stirring, but during the cooking process shake pot from side to side several times to avoid breaking the fish. Serve hot. Serves 3-4.

Greek Wedding Traditions and Customs

"SOMETHING old, something new, something borrowed and something blue" may be the primary requisites for June brides, but when a girl marries in the Greek Orthodox church she is deluged with customs and traditions which must be observed to assure a happy married life for the couple.

Up until a few years ago, when more modern customs have invaded the church ceremony, it was customary for the priest to greet the couple at the church door, and accompany them down the aisle to the altar. However, keeping up with progress, the groom now meets his bride at the steps of the altar, takes her by the arm, and begins a tour of the icons placed about the altar, which the couple kiss and bless themselves after each one.

Lasting from 45 minutes to one hour, the Orthodox ceremony presents a sharp contrast to the snappy Protestant ceremonies. By the time it is over, the couple may feel that the knot has been securely tied with no loopholes.

The first part of the ceremony is the actual engagement ceremony, which is consumated by the exchanging of the rings, in a double ring ceremony. The ring is placed on the bride's finger by the priest then on the groom's finger, and they are interchanged three times from one hand to the other.

The best man who carries the title "koumbaro" at these weddings, also goes through the ring changing process, and if there is a "koumbara", (usually the matron of honor) she also does likewise.

Rings are always worn on the right hand, unlike the customary third-finger left hand which is practiced generally with brides and grooms.

Persons acting as "Koumbaro" or Koumbara" are always called upon to act as godparents to the first child born to the couple.

At a given point in the ceremony, the bride very delicately steps upon the foot of her husband-to-be. Not that she disapproves of the goings on, but to signify that she intends to keep him underfoot during their married life.

At the conclusion of the ring ceremony, the actual wedding ceremony begins. At this point, the congregation settles back with a sigh, for the halfway mark has been reached.

Wreaths of waxen orange blossoms, joined by a white satin ribbon are placed upon the heads of the couple by the priest. These are also switched back and forth three times from the bride's head to the groom's head, in the same manner as the rings. The three changes are symbolic of the Father, Son and Holy Ghost.

The group moves around a large table set in the center of the church, pausing as each round is completed for a blessing and incantations of the choristers. This is also done three times, continuing the triad symbolism.

During these rounds, the couple is showered with rice and Jordan almonds, the latter are used to wish sweetness upon the future life of the pair, although somewhat painful if properly aimed.

Each guest, at the conclusion of the ceremony receives a "koofeta" which is a handful of Jordan almonds tied in white net and satin ribbons. These are good luck tokens which young girls sleep upon to dream of the man they will marry, much as the Anglo-Saxon girls sleep upon the bride's cake.

The passing of a cup of wine to the couple and members of the wedding party winds up the ceremony. After the "koumbaro" takes a sip, it is customary to slap him on the back of the neck for good luck. If he is unmarried the slap signifies that he will be the next to marry.

Many years ago, as a few old-timers can testify, it was customary to break a dish on the back of the "koumbaro's" head. However, a few over-zealous well-wishers caused this custom to be abandoned.

While the ceremony is in progress, it is customary for some member of the family to remain at the house to keep the house open, and welcome the couple back after the ceremony. It is considered ill luck for them to return to an empty house. Often a close friend takes over this duty.

Greek weddings are noted for their lavish and festive receptions which follow. Food, laughter, music and gaiety are combined to make the send-off of the happy couple complete up to the last moment.

GREEK PASTRIES

To those who are not acquainted with the Greek kitchen, it may be well to explain here that the pastries for which the Greeks are famous are not used for desserts as pastries are used in the Anglo-Saxon homes.

To the Greek people dessert will consist of an apple, an orange or a banana and ofttimes a mixed bowl of sliced fresh fruits. Dessert is not necessarily a part of the Greek menu.

The rich pastries in the foregoing section are reserved for guests and for special occasions. It is understandable when one realizes how rich they are, that people when they first eat them exclaim, "Goodness, how can the Greek people stand to eat such rich things for desserts!"

The majority of the recipes are topped off with a rich syrup made from sugar and water, and poured over the finished pastry. Most of them must stand twenty-four hours before serving, in order that the peak of flavor may be realized.

Namesake days of the male members of the Greek family are synonymous with the serving of rich pastries to callers. No well-reared Greek hostess would allow visitors to leave the house without first serving them a bit of pastry, thick preserves and a glass of water.

There are pastries for every holiday and occasion, and all of them are rich in many ingredients. At first most of them may seem difficult to prepare, but after a few attempts are made, and the lucious pastries merge mouth-watering and tempting, the effort is well worth the result.

POWDERED SUGAR PARTY CAKES
"Kourambiathes"

To those familiar with the Greek kitchen, perhaps no other pastry is so well known as the Kourambiathes. These crisp, crumbly cakes, rolled over and over in powdered sugar are a tradition among the Greek people, and are known as the wedding cake at all Greek Orthodox weddings.

No matter how many tiered wedding cakes may be on hand, the Kourambiathes are always served as a good luck token. Likewise they turn up at baptisms, engagement parties, birthday parties and other celebrations. It can truly be called the national Greek cake. It lasts for months without losing its flavor. To eat one without getting the sugar on the front of your dress or suit is truly a task, but the delicious taste lingers long after the sugar has been brushed away.

1 lb. butter	¼ cup powdered sugar
¾ cup nuts chopped fine	6 cups flour sifted
1 egg yolk	Whole cloves

Melt butter over medium flame, bring to boil and stir occasionally. Remove and allow to stand until salt forms a scum on top. Remove scum carefully with spoon. If butter is not clear of salt, allow to boil for one minute more. Again skim off top scum. Butter must be very clear for success with the recipe.

Slowly turn butter into mixing bowl, allowing salt particles in bottom to remain. Add powdered sugar, egg yolk and cream for 2 minutes. Add flour gradually, mixing constantly. Knead vigorously for about 30 minutes. At this point the dough should be crumbly but smooth. Add nuts and continue kneading until nuts are thoroughly mixed into dough.

Pinch off small amounts at a time, and form into half moon shapes, heart shapes or star shapes. Center each one with a clove bud.

Place on cookie sheet about ¾ inches apart. Bake in oven 375° until golden brown, for about 45 minutes.

Sift powdered sugar into large bowl and when cakes are done, roll in sugar carefully until well coated.

Arrange on platter and sift remaining sugar over them, being sure they are heavily coated.

Makes 4 dozen.

GREEK BOWKNOTS
"Diples No. 1"

One of the favorite Greek pastries are these crisp, yellow bits of pastry, which are tied in loops and fried to a crunchy consistency in hot olive oil. They are not as rich as the other Greek pastries, and are a favorite with the Greek children, and are often used as birthday cakes for children. In some parts of Greece they are called "Xerotigana" and in other parts "Kookootakya" and "Diples." But no matter what they are called, they still rank high in the Greek kitchen.

6 eggs	4 cups olive oil for frying.
2¾ cups flour	1 tsp. vanilla
⅓ cup olive oil	

Beat eggs well with vanilla and add flour slowly, kneading lightly. Add olive oil and mix well until blended. Separate dough into 5 sections. Roll one part on floured board until paper thin, keeping remainder of dough covered until ready to use to avoid drying out.

With pastry wheel, cut into strips of 2 inches wide and the length of the pastry. Form into looped bows. Drop into hot olive oil until golden brown on both sides. Be sure oil is extremely hot, so that pastry will rise properly.

Do not use frying pan for this. Best results are obtained by using deep saucepan.

Drain on absorbent paper. Sprinkle with cinnamon and powdered sugar and finely chopped nuts. Makes 3 dozen.

CREAM OF WHEAT CRISPIES

"Diples No. 2"

6 cups cream of wheat	3 cups olive oil
10 eggs	Juice of 4 oranges
½ tsp. salt	½ cup sesame
3 cups chopped pecans	

Beat eggs until light and fluffy and add cream of wheat, salt and orange juice. Knead until a smooth ball is ob-

Greek Pastries

tained. Dough should be firm but not hard. If too hard add a little water. Knead for 30 minutes.

Cut dough into 5 sections. Roll on well floured board until wafer thin. Cut with pastry cutter into strips 10 inches long and 1 inch wide. Tie in bowknots.

Fry in hot olive oil for 4 minutes or until golden brown. Drain and sprinkle with nuts, sesame and serve. Follow instructions for Diples No. 1 (above).

MILK PIE

"Galatobouryko"

½ lb. pastry sheets
2 quarts milk
½ cup cream of wheat
6 eggs slightly beaten
1 tsp. vanilla

2 cups sugar
3 tbsp. cornstarch dissolved in ½ cup cold water
½ stick butter
½ tsp. cinnamon

Boil milk and add cream of wheat, slowly and boil until thick. Add this mixture slowly to beaten eggs. Add the cornstarch solution. Stir well. Replace on fire and bring to boil. Stir for 2 minutes. Remove and add vanilla, butter, cinnamon and sugar. Set aside to cool.

Grease a 9 x 14 pan with butter generously. Place one layer of pastry sheets, covering the sides of pan, and brush with butter. Continue placing pastry sheets and butter until ¾ of sheets are used. Spread the cooled custard filling and turn in the outer layers of the sheets. Place buttered layers on filling until all are used.

Bake in oven 350° until evenly browned. Remove from oven and pour over all, syrup made from 1½ cups sugar and 1 cup of water, boiled to a medium consistency, then add juice of ½ lemon to syrup. Serves 10-12.

BAKED MILK CUSTARD
"Galatobouryko No. 2"

10 egg yolks	2 lbs. pastry sheets
¾ cup flour	1 cup butter
2¼ cups sugar	1 tsp. vanilla
6 cups milk	

Mix egg yolks, flour and sugar thoroughly, then gradually add milk and vanilla.

Cook over medium flame for 20 minutes or until smooth custard is formed, stirring constantly. Set aside to cool.

Melt butter and brush pan 9 x 13. Arrange half of pastry sheets in pan, brushing each one with butter. Pour in custard mixture and top with remaining pastry sheets. Brush top with butter and bake in moderate oven for 35 minutes. Serves 10-12.

HONEY PUFFS
"Loukoumades"

2 cups flour	1 tsp. salt
2 cups water	Rind of one lemon
⅓ cup butter	8 large eggs
5 cups cooking oil for frying	1½ cups honey
	Cinnamon

Boil water, butter and lemon rind in a large skillet for 2 minutes. Remove from heat and remove lemon rind. Add flour and salt all at once and stir vigorously. Cook over medium flame stirring constantly until mixture forms a large ball that does not separate. This takes about 5 minutes. Remove from fire and cool to lukewarm. Add eggs, one at a time beating thoroughly after each one. Continue beating until mixture is smooth.

Drop from a teaspoon into very hot olive oil and cook until golden brown for 8-10 minutes. For best results use deep saucepan.

Remove and drain on absorbent paper. Dilute honey with water to taste and pour over honey puffs. Sprinkle generously with cinnamon and serve hot. Powdered sugar may be substituted for the honey. Makes 55.

SOUR MILK POPOVERS
"Loukoumades" No. 2

2 cups Greek sour milk (Yiaourti)
3 cups flour
1/3 cup brandy
1 tsp. baking soda
2 quarts olive oil
2 cups olive oil for dipping pastry

Place milk into large bowl, and gently blend in flour. Dilute soda in brandy and add to flour and milk, mixing well.

Gently form medium soft dough, which can be easily molded. Cover with a woolen cloth and allow to stand in warm place for two hours.

Break off pieces the size of an egg and dip into cold olive oil, one at a time. Fry in deep saucepan with olive oil which is very hot. Brown balls well, and remove, drain on absorbent paper.

Prepare syrup as follows:

2 cups sugar, 1 cup water and 1/2 tsp. lemon juice.

Boil for 10 minutes, cool and pour over loukoumades. Sprinkle with cinnamon and serve hot.

GREEK SUGAR CAKE

"Ravani"

1 lb. sugar	¾ lb. butter
7 eggs separated	1 lb. rice flour
1 tsp. lemon extract	

Cream butter and sugar thoroughly with mixer for approximately 5 minutes. Add egg yolks, flavoring and flour and mix well.

Whip egg white until stiff and combine with first mixture. Pour into buttered pan 9 x 12 and bake in moderate oven 30 minutes.

Top with sliced pineapple or cherries.

WALNUT HONEY CAKE

"Karidopita"

6 eggs	½ tsp. salt
1 cup sugar	½ tsp. cinnamon
1 cup sifted flour	½ tsp. cloves
2 heaping tsp. baking powder	1 lb. walnuts chopped fine

Sift together, flour, baking powder, salt and spices. Whip egg whites until stiff and add sugar gradually continuing beating, then add egg yolks. Fold in sifted ingredients and nuts and mix well.

Bake in a pan 9 x 13 in oven 350° for 35 minutes.

While still hot top with syrup made as follows:

2 cups honey   2 cups sugar   5½ cups water

Boil sugar and water for 10 minutes to make thin syrup then add honey and cool. Pour over cake slowly. Serves 24.

GREEK HOLIDAY BREAD

1 lb. butter
12 eggs
3 cups sugar
4 yeast cakes
Flour as needed
1 tsp. baking powder

3 potatoes boiled
1 cup milk
1 cup cinnamon water (made by boiling 1 cup water with two cinnamon sticks 5 minutes)

Mix butter and sugar well, then add beaten eggs, blending thoroughly. Dissolve yeast in milk and add to first mixture, then add potatoes which have been mashed well. Mix thoroughly and begin adding flour until dough which can be easily handled is formed. Knead for a few minutes until smooth, place in greased baking pan, cover and allow to rise in warm place until double in size. Brush top with beaten egg yolk. Garnish with walnuts or Easter eggs, according to the season.

Bake in oven 350° for one hour. Four medium size loaves may be made from this recipe.

This holiday bread is a favorite in the Greek household at Christmas time, when walnuts are used as decorations and at Easter time when bright red eggs are placed in the dough, and baked with the bread. Tiny loaves may be made for the children of the family, decorating them with one egg or a few walnuts.

SESAME TURNOVERS

"Cretekia Patoutha"

2 lbs. walnuts ground fine
1 lb. almonds ground fine
1 cup sesame seeds
1 tsp. mastihi (Greek gum) mashed
1½ tsp. baking powder
Honey to blend

Mix all of above ingredients except honey. Add enough

honey to blend mixture well. Set aside and prepare pastry as follows:

- 1½ cups olive oil
- 1 cup water
- ½ tsp. mastihi mashed fine
- ½ tsp. baking powder
- 3 cups flour
- ¾ tbsp. salt
- ½ cup sugar
- Juice of one lemon
- ½ cup orange juice

Mix all ingredients together except flour, then gradually add flour forming dough that will not be sticky. Roll dough out to ⅓ inch in thickness on a board sprinkled with cornstarch.

Cut dough in 6-inch circles and place a tablespoon of the nut mixture in center. Fold over as for turnovers, pressing edges of dough together. Bake in a greased pan for approximately 15 minutes in oven 300°.

Remove from oven, and if desired, dip into rose water while still warm and sprinkle generously with powdered sugar. (The rose water is optional). Serves 20-30.

ALMOND CRISPIES

"Megthalota"

- 2 lbs. almonds chopped fine
- 1½ cups sugar
- 4 egg whites
- 2 tbsp. rose water

Mix sugar and almonds. Beat egg whites until stiff and fold in the almonds and sugar. Blend together and add rose water.

Drop by tsp. on a greased cookie sheet and bake in an oven 300° for 15 minutes. Makes approximately 25-30.

SOUR CREAM CAKE

"Yaourtini"

1 cup butter	1 cup yaourti (clabber)
2 cups sugar	2 tsp. baking soda diluted
6 eggs well beaten	with 2 oz. cognac
1 cup almonds chopped fine	2 cups flour
1 tsp. cinnamon	1 tsp. cloves

Melt butter and allow to cool slightly. Beat butter and add sugar gradually, beating thoroughly. Add eggs and continue beating. Add almonds, yaourti, soda, cognac, flour, cinnamon and cloves and beat well.

Pour into pan 9 x 13 which has been greased with butter. Bake in oven 350° for one hour.

When cool top with syrup made from 3 cups sugar and 2 cups water which has been boiled to form a syrup. Pour slowly over cake while warm. Serves 15-20.

PASTRY AND NUT TRIANGLES

"Trigona"

18 pastry sheets	6 Zwieback slices
1½ lbs. chopped almonds	½ lb. walnuts chopped fine
1 cup sugar	3 cups butter
6 eggs	1 tsp. cinnamon

Grind nuts and Zwieback together, mix well and add sugar and cinnamon. Then add melted butter; beat eggs until light and fluffy and add to nut mixture.

Cut each pastry sheet in half, using one-half for each trigona. Fold this half in thirds lengthwise, brushing with melted butter in between folds. Place a teaspoon of the nut mixture at one end and fold the filo in a triangle shape, continuing in this manner down the entire length of the filo. Place each trigona in buttered pan or cookie sheet about ½ inch apart, brush with melted butter.

Bake in oven 350° for 50 minutes. When trigona are done, remove from oven and allow to cool slightly. Prepare syrup as follows:

5 cups sugar   4 cups water   1 small slice lemon

Boil these ingredients for 10 minutes and remove from heat.

Dip each trigona into the syrup and allow to remain for 2 or 3 minutes. Arrange on large platter. Makes 36.

GREEK PASTRY
"Filo"

2¾ cups flour   1¼ cups water   3 tsp. salt

Combine ingredients and mix thoroughly, until dough becomes firm. Knead generously until the dough is smooth and easy to handle.

Sprinkle board with cornstarch and place dough on it, then sprinkle dough with flour lightly. Cover with a cloth and let stand for 50 minutes.

At the end of this time, toss dough onto a table covered with a cloth and working from the center, begin stretching dough out to the edges. Dough will stretch easily and become tissue thin. It may be stretched to cover the entire top of the table, if handled deftly and cautiously.

It takes considerable practice to become expert with this method of handling the dough, however, once it is mastered, preparing filo will be easy.

After the dough is stretched the entire amount possible without splitting, it is left to stiffen at room temperature. When the sheet begins to feel like paper, it is ready to be cut into the desired lengths to fit the pan in which it will be used.

Many sheets may be made at a time, and kept for future use.

SHREDDED WHEAT CAKE
"Kataife"

3 lbs. shredded wheat (Kataife)
6 cups walnuts chopped fine
2 teaspoons cinnamon
1½ lbs. sweet butter melted

Spread out half of the shredded wheat on a greased pan, 9 x 13, and pour half melted butter over it. Mix nuts and cinnamon together and sprinkle over shredded wheat. Add the remainder of the ingredients, and pour remainder of butter over top. Bake for 45 minutes in oven 300°.

Top with syrup made from 6 cups sugar, 3½ cups water and juice of one lemon which has been cooked for 20 minutes. Allow to cool before pouring over kataife. Cool before serving. Serves 10-12.

TURKISH DELIGHTS
"Lekoumi"

2 tbsp. unflavored gelatin
½ cup boiling water
2 cups sugar
½ cup cold water
¼ tsp. salt

Dissolve gelatin in cold water. Mix sugar, salt and boiling water and add gelatin, stirring until completely dissolved. Simmer for 20 minutes, stirring constantly. Add flavoring and pour into oblong pan and chill until firm.

Loosen edges with a wet knife and place on board which

has been sprinkled with confectioner's sugar. Cut into cubes and roll in sugar.

GREEK EASTER COOKIES
"Koulourakia"

⅓ cup butter
⅓ cup milk
2 tsp. baking powder
2 eggs

½ cup sugar
4 cups sifted flour
1 tsp. vanilla

Cream sugar, butter and vanilla thoroughly. Add 1 egg at a time beating well after each addition. Add milk and flour alternately, beating vigorously until well blended. Work with hands until a smooth dough is obtained. Sprinkle flour on board before rolling.

Break off a small portion at each time, and roll out into 6-inch rolls with hands. Form into circles and press ends together. If preferred, sesame seeds may be sprinkled on the board and rolled into the dough as the rolls are formed.

Brush tops of cookies with beaten egg and bake in greased cookie sheet for 20 minutes in oven 400°. Makes 28 cookies.

GREEK ANGEL FOOD CAKE
"Pantespani"

12 eggs
2¼ cups sugar
3¾ cup flour

6 cups sugar
6 cups water
Juice from 1 lemon
} for syrup

Beat sugar and eggs thoroughly 15-20 minutes until light and fluffy. Sift flour and fold slowly into mixture.

Grease tube pan 10 x 15 with olive oil and pour mixture slowly. Bake in oven 350° for 1 hour.

Top with syrup made from above ingredients, which

has been boiled for 15 minutes until thick. Pour slowly until all is absorbed.

Allow to cool before serving. Serves 15-20.

SPICE BARS

"Finikia"

½ cup sugar
½ cup orange juice
2 cups vegetable oil
2 tsp. cinnamon
¼ tsp. nutmeg
7 cups flour
2 cups chopped pecans

Blend vegetable oil, sugar and seasonings. Add orange juice. Add flour until a smooth dough is formed. Knead gently then add nuts.

Pinch off small portions of dough and form into little oblong rolls.

Place on greased pan and bake in oven 375° for 35 minutes.

When well browned remove from oven. While still warm dip into syrup made as follows:

2 cups honey and 1 cup water

Dip Finikia into syrup but do not alow to become soggy. Place on large platter and allow to cool. Keep syrup warm during dipping process. Makes 40-50 pieces.

ALMOND CAKE

"Megthaloto"

1 lb. pastry sheets
1½ lbs. almonds (5 cups) chopped
3 cups sugar
2 cups lunch biscuit crumbs
1 dozen eggs
1½ sticks butter

Blanch almonds, chop fine and mix with biscuit crumbs. Beat eggs and add sugar, gradually continue beating. Add almond mixture and mix thoroughly. Melt butter over low flame. Brush pan 17 x 12 generously with butter.

Arrange half of pastry sheets in bottom of pan, brushing every other one with butter. Pour in filling and arrange remainder of sheets on top, also brushing every other one with butter. Bake in oven 350° for 45-50 minutes.

Make syrup as follows: 4 cups sugar and 1½ cups water with 1 slice lemon added. Boil for 15 minutes. Cool and pour over almond cake while it is still warm. Let stand overnight before serving. Approximately 25 pieces.

BAKED CREAM OF WHEAT
"Potinga"

1 qt. milk	1 tsp. vanilla
1 cup sugar	¾ cup cream of wheat
½ cup butter	1 tsp. cinnamon
5 eggs	⅓ cup pecans chopped fine

Place milk, butter and sugar into large saucepan. Bring to boil over high flame. Gradually add cream of wheat, stirring constantly. When it begins to bubble, remove from flame immediately.

Cool for 15 minutes stirring occasionally to avoid crusting.

Beat eggs well and add to mixture. Pour into greased buttered 12 x 8 baking dish and bake for 35 minutes in 375° oven.

Remove and top with syrup made as follows:

1 cup sugar and 1 cup water brought to a boil.

Allow to cool for three hours before serving. May be garnished with chopped nuts and cherries. Serves 15 pieces.

Greek Pastries

ALMOND PIE
"Megthalopita"

½ stick butter (measure then melt) 1½ tbsp. cracker meal
½ cup sugar   or bread crumbs
1 tsp. baking powder   1 cup ground almonds
1 tbsp. flour   3 eggs well beaten

Cream sugar and butter well. Mix all dry ingredients and add to butter mixture. Add eggs and mix well. Pour into large 9-inch pie plate. Bake in moderate oven 30 minutes until lightly brown.

Make syrup of 1 cup sugar and 1 cup water. Boil 15 minutes and pour over cake slowly while still hot, until it is all absorbed. Allow to cool before serving. Cut in pie slices. Serves 6.

ZWIEBACK AND NUT CAKE
"Savarina"

6 eggs   ½ tsp. cinnamon
6 tbsp. sugar   ½ tsp. cloves
6 tbsp. Zwieback crumbs   ⅓ cup chopped pecans

Mix together cinnamon, cloves and Zwieback crumbs. Beat eggs well and add sugar continuing beating until all is well blended. Add first mixture and nuts. Mix thoroughly. Pour into well greased pan 12 x 8 and bake for 30 minutes in 350° oven, watching carefully so it will not scorch. While still hot top with syrup prepared as follows:

1½ cups sugar and ⅔ cup water boiled for 15 minutes.

Let stand 6 hours before cutting for better flavor. Serves 15.

ZWIEBACK DELIGHT
"Plakountio"

1 quart milk	1 box Zwieback crumbs (2 cups)
2 cups sugar	1 tbsp. vanilla
6 eggs	Butter for greasing pan

Beat eggs and sugar thoroughly. Add milk and beat lightly. Add Zwieback crumbs and mix well. Pour mixture into well greased pan 8 x 12. Bake in oven 375° for 30-35 minutes until golden brown.

Cut into diamond shapes and when serving garnish each piece with a cherry. Serves 20.

CHEESE CAKE
"Tiropita"

1½ cups grated cheese	1½ cups cake flour
½ cup milk	3 tsp. baking powder
½ cup butter	7 eggs well beaten

Cream butter thoroughly; add eggs, cheese and milk, mixing thoroughly after each addition. Add flour and baking powder and mix well.

Pour mixture into well greased baking pan 8½ x 8½. Bake in oven 375° for 20-25 minutes until golden brown. Cool and cut into 2-inch squares before serving. Serves 16.

BAKED HALVAH
"Halva tou Fournou"

5 eggs	½ cup cream of wheat
2 cups sugar	1 cup butter
1 tsp. baking powder	

Melt butter over low flame. Beat eggs lightly, add sugar continuously beating, add melted butter, cream of wheat and baking powder. Mix thoroughly. Pour into 12 x 8 pan and bake for 40 minutes in oven 350°. Cool for 15 minutes then proceed as follows:

Prepare syrup from 2 cups milk, ½ cup sugar which has been cooked 5 minutes. Pour slowly over pastry so it may absorb it completely. Cut into squares or diamond shapes and serve. Serves 15.

HALVAH
"Cream of Wheat Squares"

1 cup cream of wheat	½ tsp. cinnamon
1 cup milk	2½ cups sugar
½ cup butter	2½ cups water
½ cup chopped almonds or pecans	

Heat butter in skillet for about 2 minutes, then add nuts and brown lightly for 3 minutes. Add cream of wheat, stirring constantly for 4 minutes. Add milk slowly.

In the meantime bring to a boil the syrup made from the sugar and water, and allow to boil for 15 minutes. Add cream of wheat to the syrup. Cover and cook 10 minutes stirring occasionally.

Pour into 8 x 10 pyrex dish. Cool 5 minutes, sprinkle generously with cinnamon. Cool for 5 hours before cutting into squares. Serves 16.

GREEK RICE PUDDING
"Rizogolo"

1 quart milk	¼ cup butter
¼ cup rice	3 eggs
5 tbsp. sugar	⅓ cup water
1 slice of lemon	Cinnamon

Boil rice in water over high flame until it reaches the

boiling point, then lower heat and cook on medium until rice absorbs all of water. Add milk, sugar, butter and lemon.

Over high flame let come to a boil. Lower to medium and cook for 40 minutes stirring occasionally. Remove from fire. Beat eggs well with rotary beater for 8 minutes. Add to mixture slowly, and beat for 2 minutes longer. Replace on stove and continue beating. Cook 2 minutes longer.

Pour into individual custard cups, sprinkle with cinnamon and serve cold. Serves 10.

CRUNCH PASTRY ROLLS

"Bourekakia"

1 cup chopped nuts (pecans or walnuts)	1/3 tsp. nutmeg
	1/2 cup sugar
1 cup Zwieback crumbs	1 cup butter melted
1 tsp. cinnamon	18 pastry sheets

Mix dry ingredients well. Cut sheets into 16 x 10 sizes. Taking one sheet at a time, brush generously one-half of the sheet with butter. Fold over lengthwise until edges meet. Brush again with butter. Sprinkle with 1 tsp. nut mixture. Bring outer lengthwise edges together, form into rolls and place in baking dish. Continue until all sheets and ingredients are used.

Brush top generously with remaining butter. Bake in oven 375° for 35 minutes.

Prepare syrup of 1½ cups sugar and ¾ cup water and one slice of lemon. Bring to boil, then pour over rolls and allow to stand several hours before serving. Serves 16-18.

PECAN BARS
"Karithata"

2 cups butter (1 lb.)	4 cups flour
8 tbsp. powdered sugar	2 tbsp. vanilla
4 cups chopped pecans	2 tbsp. ice water

1 lb. powdered sugar

Cream butter thoroughly and add 8 tbsp. sugar and continue creaming until all is blended. Mix nuts and flour and add to cream mixture, adding gradually until well blended. Add vanilla and ice water and mix.

Roll pieces of dough with palm of hand into 1-inch rolls or half moon designs. Bake on cookie sheets for 35 minutes in oven 350° until golden brown.

Sift powdered sugar generously over rolls and place in cookie can to preserve. Arrange in layers carefully to avoid breaking. Makes 50-55.

NUT AND PASTRY ROLLS
"Saragli"

18 pastry sheets 12 x 12	1 tsp. cinnamon
2 cups chopped nuts	1 cup butter

½ cup powdered sugar

Divide pastry sheets and using 9 of them and one cup of nuts, begin by sprinkling nuts on one sheet, lay another sheet on nut mixture, continue until all are used, ending with pastry sheet.

Roll tightly lengthwise and slice in 1½-inch rolls. Arrange in baking dish tightly. Melt butter and pour 1 tbsp. over each roll.

Bake in oven 375° for ¾ hour until golden brown.

Pour syrup made from 2 cups sugar and 1 cup water

boiled 10 minutes, over rolls and let stand 2 hours before turning rolls over and allow to stand for 2 more hours before serving.

Arrange on large platter and sprinkle with powdered sugar and cinnamon sifted together. Serve 16.

ALMOND CAKE

"Kopinhain"

4⅓ cups almonds chopped fine (1 lb.)	6 Zwieback slices
1 tsp. nutmeg	1 tbsp. cognac
1 tsp. cinnamon	4 cups flour
1½ lbs. powdered sugar	1 heaping tsp. baking powder
1 cup butter	12 eggs separated

The recipe is divided into two basic parts as follows:

Part 1: Sift sugar into large bowl. Melt butter and add egg yolks one at a time beating thoroughly after each addition. Add half of the sifted sugar to this mixture and blend well.

Gradually add flour, mixing constantly. Add baking powder and mix until smooth dough is obtained. Knead lightly for about 5 minutes. Roll out to fit pan 17 x 12 allowing for the dough to be pressed firmly into the bottom of the pan and extending ½ inch over the edges.

Part 2: Mix chopped almonds, Zwieback crumbs, cinnamon and nutmeg into a large bowl. In another bowl add remaining sugar to remaining egg yolks, mixing constantly until well blended. Add cognac and mix well. Beat egg whites until stiff and gently fold into egg mixture, then add nut mixture slowly, blending well.

Pour this mixture into crust made in first mixture. If

crust stands higher than nut mixture, press firmly to even with filling.

Preheat oven to 350° and bake for 10 minutes so it will not burn. Reduce heat to 275°. Cook 25 minutes. One method of protecting the pastry is to cut a piece of white shelf paper big enough to cover the top of the pastry, and after the first 10 minutes of cooking is over, place paper over pastry and continue cooking.

While cake is baking, prepare syrup from 2 cups sugar, 2 cups water which is boiled for 15 minutes over a high flame.

When pastry is done, remove paper and pour syrup slowly over the cake, so it will absorb easily. Let stand for 7 hours before cutting or serving. Cut into diamond shapes to serve. Makes 24 pieces.

GREEK JELLY ROLL

"Kormos"

3 eggs	Grated rind of one lemon
1 cup flour	3 tsp. sugar
1 cup jelly (any kind preferred)	½ tsp. soda

Beat yolks and white of eggs separately, then add sugar to the yolks, and beat until glossy and stiff. Add soda and lemon rind, flour and fold in stiff egg whites.

Grease 9 x 12 pan and line with waxed paper. Pour mixture into pan and bake in moderate oven for 10 minutes. Remove from pan, and spread with jelly. Roll while warm and sprinkle with powdered sugar. Slice to serve.

FRUIT NUT CUSTARD

"Gleko Krema"

4 cups milk	1 cup crystallized fruit chopped fine
6 tsp. cornstarch	
1 cup sugar	1 cup peanuts, roasted and chopped
3 egg yolks	

Beat egg yolks until fluffy, then add sugar and continue beating. Dissolve cornstarch in half cup milk and add to remainder of milk then boil until a smooth custard is formed, add first ingredients and cook until smooth. Add fruits and nuts. Pour into custard cups and serve cold. Serves 6-7.

BAKLAVA

1 lb. butter	¼ cup lemon juice
1 lb. pastry sheets	2 lb. sugar
1 lb. blanched almonds	2 tsp. all-spice
½ tsp. cinnamon	1 tsp. nutmeg

Chop almonds very fine and add spices and ½ cup sugar and mix well in large bowl.

Melt butter, removing salt scum which forms on top, until butter is clear. Brush bottom of pan 9 x 12 with melted butter and place 4 pastry sheets in pan. Brush these sheets with butter and spread nut mixture on every other layer, until all ingredients are used, ending with 4 layers. Brush top with butter and cut into diamond shapes, placing 1 clove bud in center of each diamond.

Bake for 1½ hours in oven 300° until lightly brown.

Prepare syrup with two parts sugar and 1 part water, cook until it spins in a fine thread when dropped from spoon and add lemon juice.

Greek Pastries

Remove pastry from oven and pour syrup over it, while both are still hot. Allow to stand 24 hours before serving.

BAKLAVA

14 pastry sheets	1 tsp. cinnamon
4 cups chopped pecans	Grated rind of one orange
1¼ cups sugar	1 cup butter

Mix nuts, sugar, cinnamon and orange rind well. Melt butter and brush well a pan 13 x 9. Place one layer (2 sheets) in bottom of baking pan and allow ends to extend over pan. Sprinkle heavily with nut mixture, and place two layers over this. Brush these layers with butter and sprinkle nut mixture. Alternate in this manner until all ingredients and sheets have been used, ending with 2 pastry sheets.

Brush top with remaining butter and trim edges with sharp knife. Cut through top with diagonal lines to form diamond shapes.

Bake in oven 375° for one hour until light brown, watching carefully so it will not burn.

While still hot cover with syrup and let stand overnight before serving.

Prepare syrup with 2 cups water, 3 cups sugar and 1 tsp. lemon juice. Combine these ingredients and boil for 10 minutes. Serves 24.

NUT TORTE

"Melahrino"

2 cups crushed Zwieback crumbs	½ tsp. salt
2 cups chopped pecans	1 cup sugar
2 tsp. vanilla	6 eggs separated
½ tsp. cinnamon	2 tsp. baking powder

Mix dry ingredients thoroughly then add vanilla. Beat

egg yolks until light, add sugar and beat again until a light lemoon color is obtained. Add to dry ingredients, mixing thoroughly.

Beat egg whites until stiff, and fold into mixture. Pour into greased pan 8 x 12. Bake in oven 325° for 30 minutes.

When done and still hot, top with syrup made as follows:

4 cups water and 3 cups sugar boiled 30 minutes.

Pour the syrup over the torte slowly so it may be completely absorbed. Let stand 6 hours before serving. Serves 24.

GREEK COFFEE RECIPE

GREEK COFFEE

4 demi-tasse cups water   4 heaping tsp. Greek coffee
4 tsp. sugar

To be properly prepared, this coffee must be cooked in a special bronze coffee-pot, which is a "must" in every Greek kitchen. It is customary to serve this coffee to guests in the afternoons, as a pick-up before dinner time. May be served at the conclusion of a meal also. To be appreciated, it must be sipped slowly, giving the flavor time to settle. Thick grounds remain in the bottom of the cup, which are used to read fortunes by those skilled in the practice.

Put water in Greek coffee-maker. Place over high flame. When water boils add sugar and stir well. Continue boiling. Add coffee, stir well and remove immediately, so as to form a heavy coat on top and to retain flavor.

Put one tsp. of the foam into each demi-tasse cup. Pour remaining coffee filling each cup.

Serve very hot. Serves 4.

INDEX TO RECIPES

Cheese and Milk Recipes   Page

    Cheeses 8
    Cheese, Cream 12
    Cheese, Baked Pie...................................... 11
    Cheese, Pudding Baked................................. 10
    Cheese, Pudding Feta................................... 11
    Clabber, Greek *(Yaourti)* 9
    Yeast for Yaourti....................................... 10

Chicken

    Chicken, Baked Greek Style.......................... 68
    Chicken, Buttered with Potatoes...................... 69
    Chicken, with Okra..................................... 68
    Chicken, with Peas..................................... 70
    Chicken, with Rice..................................... 67
    Chicken, with Spaghetti................................ 69
    Chicken, Stewed 68
    Turkey, Dodecanese Style.............................. 70

Dedication.. iii

Easter Food Customs 72

Epiphany Day... 13

Fish and Seafood Recipes

    Crabs and Rice... 76
    Cod, Fried with Garlic Dressing....................... 83
    Fish, Baked and Vegetables............................ 83
    Fish, Braised 85
    Fish, Broiled with Lemon Sauce....................... 78
    Fish, Broiled Greek Style.............................. 78
    Fish, Fried, Marinata.................................. 75
    Fish Patties 80
    Roe, Cakes 79
    Roe, Salad 76

Fish and Seafood Recipes—*Cont.*	*Page*
Scallops, with Rice	79
Shrimp, Braised	82
Shrimp, Fried Greek Style	82
Shrimp, with Rice	81
Snails, Stewed	77
Squid, Stuffed	84
Squid, with Rice	84

Greek Coffee 115

Greek Wedding Traditions and Customs 86

Herbs ix

Introduction xi

Meats

Lamb with Artichokes	52
Lamb, Baked Greek Style	44
Lamb, Braised	51
Lamb, with Cauliflower	49
Lamb, with Celery and Avgolemono Sauce	45
Lamb, Fricasseé	46
Lamb, Kabobs, No. 1	50
Lamb, Kabobs, No. 2	51
Lamb, with Okra	48
Lamb with Okra, Halki Style	52
Lamb and Rice	47
Lamb Roast with Potatoes	48
Lamb Roast with Rice	51
Lamb with String Beans	49
Lamb with Spinach	50
Lamb Stuffed, Halki Style	53
Lamb with Manestra	46
Lamb with Tomato Sauce	53
Lamb with Small Green Squash	45
Lamb with Spaghetti	44
Meat-Balls	57
Meat-Balls with Avgolemono Sauce	60
Meat-Balls, Baked	57
Meat-Balls, Baked Constantinople Style	61

Index

Meats—*Cont.* — *Page*

Hamburg Rolls	56
Keftedes (Greek Meat-Balls)	57
Meat-Balls with Manestra	62
Meat-Balls with Potatoes	54
Meat-Balls, Smyrna Style	56
Savory Side Dish	63
Spaghetti with Hamburger Sauce	59
Spaghetti and Ground Beef	58
Mousaka	61
Steak Broiled Greek Style	55
Stew, Greek Beef	55
Stew with Onions	63
Pork Roast with Potatoes	64
Pigs Feet, Halki Style	64
Rabbit Stew	65
Veal, Halki Style	65

Pastries

Almond Cake	103
Almond Cake	110
Almond Crispies	98
Almond Pie	105
Angel Food Cake (Greek)	102
Baklava	112
Baklava	113
Bowknots (diples)	91
Cheese Cake	106
Cookies, Easter	102
Cream of Wheat Crispies	92
Cream of Wheat, Baked	104
Custard, Baked Milk	94
Custard, Fruit Nut	112
Halvah	107
Halvah, Baked	106
Holiday Bread, Greek	97
Honey Puffs	94
Jelly Roll (Greek)	111
Kourambiathes	90
Milk Pie	93
Nut Torte	113

Pastries—*Cont.*   *Page*

- Nut and Pastry Rolls 109
- Pecan Bars 109
- Pastry (filo) 100
- Pastry Crunch Rolls 108
- Pastry and Nut Triangles 99
- Pudding, Rice 107
- Sesame Turnover 97
- Sour Milk Popovers 95
- Sour Cream Cake 99
- Shredded Wheat Cake 101
- Spice Bars 103
- Sugar Cake, Greek 96
- Turkish Delights 101
- Walnut Honey Cake 96
- Zwieback Delight 106
- Zwieback and Nut Cake 105

Salads

- Greek 16
- Mixed Greek 16
- Hot Potato 17
- Lima Bean 17
- Spinach 17
- Vegetable, Greek Style 18
- Dressing, Greek 18

Sauces

- Cream Sauce, No. 1 3
- Cream Sauce, No. 2 3
- Egg and Lemon Sauce 2
- Garlic Sauce 1

Soups

- Bean, White 6
- Bean, Greek 7
- Chicken with Avgolemono Sauce 4
- Easter, Greek 5
- Fish and Avgolemono Sauce 5
- Lentil 6

Superstitions xiii

Index

Vegetables

	Page
Artichokes, Fried	37
Artichokes, Halki Style	37
Artichokes with Fava Beans	38
Beans, Baked Garbanzo	33
Beans, Garbanzo with Rice	33
Beans, String, Greek Style	24
Beans, String, Halki Style	24
Cabbage, Stuffed	27
Carrots, Loaf	36
Cauliflower, Baked, with Cream Sauce	36
Eggplants, Baked	38
Eggplants, Casserole	41
Eggplants, Fried	40
Eggplant and Meat Casserole	40
Eggplant, Small Greek	39
Grapevine Leaves, Stuffed	28
Grapevine Leaves Stuffed with Rice	30
Grapevine Leaves Stuffed with Squash	29
Lentils with Egg Noodles	32
Macaroni, Baked Pastitisio	31
Okra and Tomatoes	41
Peppers Stuffed	25
Peppers Stuffed, Halki Style	25
Peppers Stuffed, Smyrna Style	25
Rice, Baked, Greek Style	34
Rice, Pilaffe	34
Spaghetti with Butter	30
Tomatoes, Stuffed, Galaxidi Style	26
Tomatoes Stuffed with Eggplants	27
Squash Baked with Cheese	22
Squash Casserole	22
Squash, Greek Style	23
Squash, Island Style	23
Squash Patties	23
Spinach Pie	19
Spinach with Rice	20
Spinach Turnovers	21

www.ingramcontent.com/pod-product-compliance
Lightning Source LLC
Chambersburg PA
CBHW071850230426
43671CB00012B/2133